GREEN
BIRDING

GREEN BIRDING

Richard Gregson

STACKPOLE BOOKS

Published by
STACKPOLE BOOKS
5067 Ritter Road
Mechanicsburg, PA 17055
www.stackpolebooks.com

Printed in China

10 9 8 7 6 5 4 3 2 1

First edition

Cover design by Tessa J. Sweigert

ISBN 978-0-8117-2615-3

This book was printed using responsible environmental practices by FSC® certified book manufacturers. The Forest Stewardship Council ™ (FSC) encourages the resonsible management of the world's forests.

Cataloging-in-Publication Data is on file with the Library of Congress

Contents

What is Green Birding?

On a bright morning in May, Samuel stepped onto the deck of his house with a coffee in one hand and his binoculars in the other to watch a Downy Woodpecker taking peanuts from a tube feeder across his lawn. A male Northern Cardinal offered seeds to his mate on the perch of a nearby silo feeder, while chickadees called busily from the shrubs, waiting for the bigger birds to move on. At the top of a maple tree in a neighbor's garden a Great Crested Flycatcher was darting out over and again from a high branch to take insects on the wing.

An hour earlier, as dawn was breaking, Samuel's friend Sally and her husband, Marc, had strapped spotting scopes and a lunch bag onto their bicycles and set off for a long day birding in their "patch," an area of nearby woodland and marsh habitats that they regularly monitor for newly arrived migratory birds and old resident friends. On these expeditions they always hope to add some "good" birds to their patch lists—and maybe, just maybe, a lifer. As they observed the birds in their patch, they recorded their sightings in notebooks and with smartphone apps. When they returned home at the end of the day, they would enter their sightings onto their computer and upload the observations to the eBird database, where they would be available to ornithologists studying changing bird populations and the factors that affect them.

Around noon, Samuel's father, David, collected his dog and a stout stick to take a half-hour prelunch stroll around his neighborhood. Not far from home he spent ten minutes watching a Merlin's nest high in a garden tree where, he knew from previous observation, young had hatched. He was pleased to see that the neighborhood cats and squirrels had left them alone for another day. At the end of the road, he heard and then saw a Tufted Titmouse in a tree near the riverside—a new bird for his locality. David had heard they were being seen in the vicinity in recent years and had long hoped to add one to his list. Later that day, back at home, he would spend a few minutes writing up his sightings in his personal bird observation records, a lifetime's activity that he could look back on.

Five miles away, four highly skilled volunteers from a migratory bird banding station were raising funds for their studies by walking local trails

The small and exquisite Verdin can be found in desert patches.

trying for a sponsored personal best Big Day list of bird species in their local area—a challenge for which they had found significant financial sponsorship from their community and friends. They were just recording their 64th species of the day, a Baltimore Oriole that they first heard singing and then, after some searching, saw high in a tree along the side of the field they were walking across.

At a nearby school, a class of tenth grade students were monitoring the breeding success of Eastern Bluebirds in nest boxes that they had installed on the school grounds. Through the project, they were learning about the bluebirds, improving their observational skills, doing some interesting basic science, and concentrating their efforts on the birds living in their area.

Samuel, Sally, Marc, David, the banders, and the school students were all "green birding." Their birding on that day included a wide range of activities, but what they all had in common is that they were all consciously avoiding the use of an internal combustion engine to get to their birding sites. Not only were they helping to reduce the greenhouse gas burden on the planet, they were seeing more birds than most people expect to be visible within human-powered reach of their homes and gaining in-depth insights into the lives of the birds that live near them. They were having a very enjoyable time too—green birding is satisfying, educational, and fun.

All over the world, birders and other wildlife watchers are becoming uncomfortable with the fact that getting to see "good" birds and adding new species to their personal life lists often entails long journeys (in some cases

The Common Raven is a wonderful bird with a wide range, appearing all over North America. This specimen was taking crabs along the shore of Vancouver Island.

even international flights)—journeys powered by internal combustion engines that churn out greenhouse gases into our already-burdened atmosphere. Mainstream birding is a wildly popular pastime and the people that enjoy it are among the most concerned members of the population when it comes to the protection of wild creatures and their habitats—but by its very nature, birding contributes to climate change, which is having a very noticeable effect on the birds we all enjoy.

A small but ever-increasing number of people are now green birding—some all the time, others for at least part of their birding activities. Green birders differ from mainstream birders in just one important way: they make a conscious decision that all, or at least most, of their birding is going to be carried out using only human power to travel from home to bird and back again. This can be as simple as out of our front doors and seeing what birds are in the front yard; biking, rowing a boat, and paddling a canoe or kayak are also forms of green birding. For some of birders it includes horse riding or even a pony and cart, if available. When you think of it, this is actually rather appealing, unless you happen to be someone who enjoys sitting in a car for hours rather than looking at birds in the open air!

Green birding started among the listers of the birding world when they decided to restrict their travel in pursuit of new species, but it doesn't stop there. Green birding is just as much—perhaps even more so—about birders taking an in-depth interest in the habitats and creatures that share their particular part of the planet. It is about truly getting to know and understand the birds that are on your personal local birding "patch," and about looking after them. In many ways, green birding is concerned with depth more than it is with breadth.

This book is about the green birding phenomenon. It has been written for both experienced and new birders, both hardcore and casual, in the hope that it will encourage you to think about doing all or most of your birding locally and under your own power by walking, cycling, or paddling. Along the way, you will discover the unexpected pleasures of getting to know your local patch better than you thought possible and learn how this concentration of your energies on a smaller area can actually increase the scientific value of your observations

Leave your car in the garage. Truly, you do not need it.

"One never knows when something will just appear, so every mile I rode my bike gave me that much more of a chance to spot something. My Big Green Big Year gave me the excuse to get on my bike to go places, be it commuting to my office or to go downtown. And that's where the real effect gets magnified if other people begin to use alternate transportation for everyday travel. If a thousand more people can ride their bikes two thousand miles a year, we'd be doing the carbon sequestering work of ten acres of forests."

—Christian Nunes, Boulder, Colorado

Why Green Birding?

GOOD FOR US

At a very basic and simple level, being a green birder means that you are getting about under your own power. You are walking, cycling, skiing, canoeing, or horseback riding quite a bit more than you would otherwise be doing. On top of that, these are all activities that most people find pleasant in and of themselves; adding some exercise on top of the birding is just icing on the cake.

But it is good for more than our figures. Green birders, because they do their birding in a more confined area than driving-birders, are compelled to spend more time getting to know their local environment in considerable depth. We find little nooks and crannies and interesting vistas that often we would otherwise totally ignore. We discover where the birds nest, and we spend more time watching them going about their business of simply being birds. There is a lot of pleasure to be had in learning about the common and commonplace as well as the exotic and rare. Not only are we doing good to our bodies by exercise, but we are also doing good to our minds and even our souls by studying the birds in our area and on our birding patches.

GOOD FOR THE ENVIRONMENT

The main reason why birders first become interested in green birding is, of course, that it is good for the environment. As our chosen pastime depends on the health of that environment, we need to take special care to make sure that the way we pursue our hobby is not harmful to the very birds we study.

At first glance it seems ridiculous to suggest that birders, of all people, are not green to the depths of their souls. After all, is not a love of birds and wildlife a sine qua non for the birding tribe? Do we not care deeply for birds and depend on their continued existence? Are we not offended by the atti-

A lake or river is a quiet, peaceful place to spend a day—and it is rich in birdlife.

tudes in society that consider environmental protection to be little more than a nice idea that can be brushed aside when there is a chance to make money by building luxury condos on a pristine riverside wetland or widen a road or cut down a forest? Many of us give money to environmental charities and we may even vote for political candidates that have a strong commitment to reducing greenhouse gas emissions and limiting city sprawl. If we look honestly at ourselves, though, we will too often see that as a group we tend to act just like the rest of the population and shut our eyes to what we, personally, can do to be more green simply because it is inconvenient. We live in the moment and forget about the future.

Not long ago on the American Birding Association's birding blog, Ted Floyd made the following observations: "Birders get around. They burn up the frequent-flier miles, they own and make frequent use of SUVs with poor fuel efficiency. They wear expensive clothes, they stay in hotels, they eat out. Birders carry expensive optics. They own lots of bird books. Birding is a hugely consumptive hobby. Birders' hearts and minds may well be 'green,' but their lifestyles are anything but."

When this lifestyle is questioned, too many birders will shrug it off with comments such as, "What can I do, I'm just one guy in millions?," "I give money to Audubon and buy carbon offsets; my conscience is clean," or "I'm a birder and the birds are widely scattered—you have to go where they are."

But there is one simple thing that we can do: try to reduce our carbon footprints as a practical contribution to reducing climate change. It's a small change, but there are an awful lot of birders around the globe, and if we all made some small changes, it would make a significant difference.

What are the environmental impacts of regular birding? It's somewhat complicated to compute, but I am going to make some conservative (and probably controversial) estimates. What follows is meant to be illustrative rather than to give precise estimates of exactly how much greenhouse gases are produced by birders birding by car and plane—it is probably impossible to get exact figures.

The first problem is that nobody knows how many birders there are, and anyway, how do you define a birder? We do know that birding is one of the most popular pastimes in North America. It is hugely popular in bird-crazy countries like the twitcher-replete United Kingdom; there are hardcore birders in most nations on the planet. But just how many? Impossible to say with certainty.

Birding at some level or another is hugely popular. Figures published by the Forest Service in their National Survey on Recreation and the Environment (NSRE) in 2006 estimated that an astonishing 81.4 million people take part in bird-watching in the U.S. and that they participated in 8.2 billion days of birding in each year. Realistically, of course, we know that serious birders, the ones likely to travel significant distances to find "good" birds, are but a fraction of this huge number, but the consensus in the birding community is that the committed birder population numbers in the "several tens of thousands."

But we are trying to make some estimates and so, for the sake of argument, let's be really conservative and say that there are only 20,000 people in North America and Europe who are truly serious about this birding game and who keep some sort of list of the birds they have seen. These are people who are members of national or local birding clubs and are interested enough to go after rarities when they come within striking distance. We will assume, not unreasonably, that they go birding twice a month and that each trip averages 50 miles by car—undoubtedly a low estimate I would say, judging from my own birding friends. Let's also assume that once every two years they take a vacation with the primary purpose of birding, in which they fly a round-trip distance of 2,000 miles. Thus our nominal population of birders in a given year drive a total of 24 million miles and fly 20 million miles.

The US Environmental Protection Agency has estimated that a typical car emits 0.9 pounds of CO_2 per mile and that a 2,000-mile medium-haul airplane journey produces 286 pounds of CO_2 per passenger. Thus in a typical year our hypothetical 20,000 really keen birders are responsible for the addition of 21.6 million pounds of CO_2 by driving and 5.7 million pounds by flying—putting a total of 27.3 million pounds, or about 9,500 tons, of carbon dioxide into the atmosphere.

And many individual birders will produce many, many times more than the average. A friend of mine drove 1,000 miles in a weekend a couple of years ago, only to *not* see a rarity that had been reported on the Gaspé Peninsula in Québec, and said that he would do it again. In fact, he has.That one fruitless expedition alone produced several hundred pounds of CO_2.

And let's not forget the more low-key bird lovers. With 81 million people taking part in bird watching, it's conservative to estimate there are one million people who are less committed to birding—they might not even call themselves "birders"—but who own binoculars and at least one field guide and "go birding," or at least go on a trip that includes looking at birds and other wildlife, ten times a year. If each of those trips includes an average driving distance of 100 miles, that's an additional 1,000 miles driven per year per person—for a total of 1,000,000,000 additional miles. This adds another 31,250 tons of CO_2.

Thus, our estimated birding population in North America is responsible for the addition of 40,750 tons of greenhouse gases into the atmosphere.

It is calculated that all the cars of the world produce some 900,000,000 tons of CO_2—a number so big it's hard to comprehend—so just what do our birders' 40,750 tons mean when weighed against that? A drop in the ocean? Not at all: every ton of CO_2 added to the atmosphere, by whatever means, is the equivalent of chopping down and burning six fully mature trees, "carbon offsets" traders have calculated. This means the carbon emissions from our birding activities in North America are equivalent to cutting and burning almost a quarter of a million (244,500) trees every year.

Or look at it this way: one acre of newly planted trees will sequester 3.67 tons of CO_2 per year for the first five years of their growth, meaning that we would have to plant 11,100 acres of new forest every year to capture the CO_2 emissions just from our birding activities. The average North American city park covers 54 acres—so our trees would need to take over the land presently occupied by 205 city parks every year. This is not at all insignificant—and not at all what is happening.

But what if there are actually 40,000, or 60,000, or 100,000 really serious birders who go out every weekend and average 75 miles per trip (or 100 or 200)? The effect of birding on our planet could be much greater than our conservative estimate. What we can know for certain is that as birders we are each producing avoidable greenhouse gas emissions that affect the climate.

But perhaps not everyone is convinced that the problem really exists. Are there not still birds in our trees and gardens and fields aplenty?

Well, not so much.

The Audubon Society's website notes:

> When it comes to global warming, birds are like canaries in the coal mine, showing us that temperature increases are reshaping our ecology in potentially dangerous ways. Nearly 60% of 305 species found in North America in winter have been on the move over the last 40 years, shifting their ranges northward by an average of 35 miles, and in some cases by hundreds of miles.

Anything that causes observable changes like this in the behaviour or distribution of such a large number of species is not something to brushed off lightly.

In the year 2000 it was estimated that some 11 percent of all bird species—that's over 1,000 species—were already at risk from climate change and that within 20 years some 200 of those species could disappear altogether—if not from the planet, at least across vast swathes of their traditional ranges. At the time of writing this book we are already over halfway to that 20-year point, and indeed, species are demonstrably disappearing from certain locations and habitats at an alarming rate—and when that happens, it affects other species as well. For example, it has been observed in Costa Rica that Rainbow-billed Toucans have moved from the lowlands to the higher-elevation cloud forests and are competing there for tree-cavity nest space with the Resplendent Quetzal and even eating their eggs. Elsewhere, rising sea levels drown the nests of ducks and other waterfowl nesting on shorelines. Many other species of mammals, insects, and plants are also being hit hard; loss of habitat and climate change are threatening their abilities to maintain viable populations.

There are not just fewer kinds of birds—there are fewer birds altogether as a result of climate change. For example, populations of Emperor Penguins in Antarctica are decreasing because of rising sea temperatures that adversely alter the availability of fish and squid during the all-important time of year when young are being raised. Closer to home, Sooty Shearwaters on the Pacific coast of North America and Atlantic Puffins on the eastern seaboard are showing huge declines in number for much the same reason. The temperature change that is driving these declines? A mere 0.7 degrees Celsius.

Climate change also affects birds' ranges—sometimes with dramatic results. Birds, like most species, are highly adapted to specific vegetation and habitat types. As temperatures increase and vegetation changes correspondingly, many species are compelled to move their ranges northwards or to higher elevations. A report published by Audubon in 2009 noted that the ranges of dozens of bird species have been shifting northward over the last forty years. Where I live in southern Quebec, Northern Cardinals were unheard of rarities twenty or thirty years ago yet now are hanging off every tree and garden feeder. Carolina Wrens and Red-bellied Woodpeckers have started to appear here in recent years and are even beginning to breed successfully, while the number of flocks of Wild Turkeys are increasing year by year (much to the delight of turkey hunters, I am sorry to say).

The timing of birds' migration, reproduction, breeding, nesting, and hatching are all highly adapted to match specific local conditions, such as the availability of suitable habitat and adequate food sources. Since climate change will affect different species differently, bird behavior may no longer be synchronized with food availability when the birds' ranges move in response to climate change. Humphrey Crick of the British Trust for Ornithology has elegantly demonstrated that birds are now responding ineffectively to climate change—and this includes not responding when they should—and are becoming out of sync with their environments.

In North America, a large proportion of our birds are long-distance migrants with breeding grounds in the boreal forests of Canada and wintering areas in the tropics and neotropics. When these birds arrive at their breeding grounds, hungry and with low fat reserves, they expect—indeed, they are dependent upon—a readily available and rich selection of insects to feed them and the young that they will shortly be raising. Because of climate changes, some of these long-distance migrant species may be arriving at their destinations at the same time of year, sometimes the same day, that they and their ancestors always have, but they are no longer arriving at the peak of insect production. The triggers for birds to migrate north are almost always seasonal changes in daylight, which are fixed and immutable. The trigger for insects to hatch, however, is usually temperature. Climate change is causing the insects of the boreal forests to hatch a couple of weeks earlier than the arrival of the birds that feed on them. Suddenly the exquisitely timed interaction that evolved between the birds and the insects is out of kilter. Those two weeks make the difference between a pair of birds being able to find enough food to raise their young and their having nestlings starve to death before they are fledged and able to forage independently. Even the bird species that eat seeds as adults need a reliable supply of insects at a critical period to feed their young in the nest.

This is not just happening in North America. In Europe, species of flycatchers that overwinter in North Africa are returning to find that peak insect production in the United Kingdom, France, and Scandinavia has passed before their arrival—resulting in marked reductions in their population because they cannot raise as many young.

On the other hand, American Robins in the Rocky Mountains have begun returning north to their breeding grounds some two weeks earlier than they did a few decades ago, spurred on by slightly higher spring temperatures in their wintering sites, but the worms and other food that they eat are not yet available for their newly hatched offspring. Why? Because a counterintuitive consequence of global warming at the moment is higher precipitation in northern latitudes—leading to deeper snow cover, which takes longer to melt in the spring. Snow and ice on the ground make the worms inaccessible to the robins. Dozens, if not hundreds, of such disjunctions in bird activity have been documented.

What about nonmigratory birds? Are they immune to the challenges their migratory relatives face?

Hardly. Gray Jays, most of which live in the boreal forests, are a nonmigratory species, but climate change is still disrupting the finely tuned lifestyle they have developed. These birds hoard food for the winter and early spring but need to have reliable freezing temperatures to keep it from spoiling. Some of this stored food will be used to get the adults through the winter and some of it is essential for feeding their young when they hatch in April. With our changing global climate, those frosts are delayed more and more, resulting in many of the food stores beginning to spoil. Studies have shown that more young survive in years following cold fall weather than warm fall weather—and climate change means a lot more warm falls.

Water birds such as ducks are also affected. It has been estimated that some 14,000,000 North American ducks are totally reliant on the boreal forests of Canada for their breeding habitat before they spread out over the rest of the continent for the rest of the year. Increasing temperatures in the north—climate change is seen in northern latitudes sooner and more intensively than further south—are causing forest ponds and wetlands to dry up and disappear; in the past fifty years, huge reductions of water surface area have been evident. Less water means fewer ducks—as simple as that. It also means fewer trees, which in turn reduces nesting opportunities for millions of smaller songbirds.

It has been calculated that significant reductions in the populations of 14 species of migratory waterfowl will be seen from southeastern Alberta and northeastern Montana to southern Manitoba and western Minnesota, with a probable 40 to 50 percent decline in the numbers of ducks that are able to raise their young in the area. From this we will see a reduction in those species all over their traditional range.

Climate change has seen birds such as the Northern Cardinal moving northward for the past couple of decades.

Another bird particularly dependent on water is the Whooping Crane, an iconic bird whose rescue from the brink of extinction has been closely followed by birders in recent years. There are still only a little under 500 of these beautiful birds in North America, all of whom breed in northern Alberta, where they make use of wetlands. In years of low rainfall, the cranes' nests too often fail—and there have been an increasing number of dry years in the critical area recently. When the birds do manage to raise young, they must then migrate south for the winter. Many head for the Aransas National Wildlife Refuge in Texas, where they feed on the blue crabs that they find in shallow coastal marshes. Global warming is slowly raising sea levels, and these important marshes are threatened by flooding, erosion, and increased salinity—all of which reduce the availability of the crabs on which the Whooping Cranes depend.

Such examples make a long, sad list. There was a 90 percent decline in Sooty Shearwaters off the California coast between 1987 and 1994 that was associated with warming of the California Current, which flows from southern British Columbia to Baja California, and consequential changes in fish populations. The Blackwater National Wildlife Refuge, an Important Bird Area in Maryland that provides essential habitat for many common and endangered species such as the Black Rail and Saltmarsh Sharp-tailed Sparrow, is expected to lose all of its wetlands within 25 years as a result of both climate change and aquifer extraction. Several of the North American warbler species have moved their ranges northward more than 65 miles, with the Golden-winged Warbler's having moved nearly 100 miles north in the past 20 years. In Michigan, 15 species of birds, such as the Rose-breasted Grosbeak and Black-throated Blue Warbler, are arriving in the spring up to 21 days earlier than they did 40 years ago. A search online will turn up many more such examples.

Other cases are even sadder and more difficult to resolve. At the southern end of the Rocky Mountains in the unsurpassed birding nirvana of Arizona are the Sky Islands. These are a series of isolated mountain ranges that rise from the surrounding desert, much as islands rise from the ocean. The Sky Islands are quite unique and contain an amazingly rich and diverse group of inhabitants. Climate change is affecting these special places with an unsettling rapidity and severity, as—just as oceans are rising and submerging coastal habitats—hotter and drier conditions are moving up the slopes of the Sky Islands. As you move up these slopes some 7,000 feet in altitude from the hot desert to the cool summits, you pass through narrow climatic zones that represent all the habitats of North America, from southern desert to boreal forests like those of Canada. Sometimes these climatic bands can occupy no

Areas such as this dry canyon in the Chiracahua Mountains, Arizona, have an avifauna found nowhere else. Sadly, not many birders live in such places—though it is amazing how far some of us green birders will travel by bicycle when the birds are waiting.

more than one or two hundred feet in altitude and each contains its very specialized and unique fauna and flora.

Matt Skroch, head of the conservation group Sky Island Alliance, has pointed out that in some of these areas about 80 percent of the pines are dead, simply because it's getting hotter. This gradual change is moving relentlessly up the mountainsides. In these circumstances the effect on birdlife can be catastrophic. As the temperatures rise and the vegetation groups move higher and higher, the available habitat for the specialized birds that need cooler conditions diminishes dramatically. Species become trapped and isolated. There is nowhere for these birds to flee to. Winged flyers they may be, but the possibility of them escaping over hundreds of miles of dry desert to light upon another welcoming habitat are effectively nonexistent. Even if the birds knew which direction to fly, the odds are stacked heavily against them surviving the heat and dryness—and even if they did arrive at a good spot, it would likely already be occupied. These birds are not going to get a second chance. We must resign ourselves to the sad fact that we are going to lose them.

All of these changes have been brought about by what to most people would seem to be a rather tiny and inconsequential rise in worldwide average temperatures of 1.3 degrees Fahrenheit above pre-industrial levels. As Terry Root, an ecologist from Stanford University, asked, "what happens when it's 5.4 degrees F? Global warming presents the greatest threat to birds and other wildlife in human history. It's an uncontrolled experiment."

And *that* is why birders should give very serious consideration to becoming green birders. We need to accept the challenge that our fascinating hobby is going to have to change, that no longer is chasing all over the planet after rare birds in greenhouse gas–emitting vehicles a sustainable way to go about pursuing an interest in birdlife. And so we must alter our habits. By making these changes willingly and openly, and challenging others to do likewise, we can demonstrate that birders, the people who are seen as in the forefront when it comes to caring about the environment, are actually doing something, however small, to ameliorate the problem.

Where we lead, others may follow.

"Yesterday I helped out with the Washington County Migration Count. I devoted my whole day to it, and did it BIGBY [Big Green Big Year] style: all on bike and on foot. I haven't added up the exact mileage, but it was over 30 miles on bike and at least 7 on foot. I went pretty much from dawn until after dark, with only 2 sizeable breaks: one in mid-morning for coffee and second breakfast, and to call my mom for Mother's Day; and another break in the afternoon for some lunch and rest. It turned into something of a Big Day, and indeed, at 109 species it was by far my biggest day yet in Arkansas, rivaling many of my single-day species lists for Florida. I birded 4 major areas: Mt. Sequoyah, Woolsey Wet Prairie, Razorback Golf-course, and Lake Wilson . . . plus a few smaller areas around my neighborhood.

Aside from the numbers, the day held many awe-inspiring moments. The dawn chorus at Mt. Sequoyah and dusk at Lake Wilson were chief among these. The trails around Lake Wilson are beautiful, with large moss-covered boulder piles and streams. One side of the lake held the vast majority of the astounding 30 Swainson's Thrushes; I was surrounded by "quip" calls and the occasional sweet fluting song. As I was watching flitting warblers high in the trees I saw my Arkansas lifer Blackburnian Warbler, lit up by the setting sun; it was so beautiful and unexpected that I actually gasped aloud. As it got dark, Common Nighthawks emerged to feed over the lake, and the voices of Chuck-will's-widows rang out among the hills. Riding back home, I saw a Chuck in the road in the beam of my bike light, and it didn't budge until I came to a squealing halt right in front of it. It flew just a little farther down the road, and sat there in my light for a few minutes before flying off. What an encounter!"

—Abigail Darrah (post on www.birdforum.net)

Getting Started

2

THREE PARTS OF GREEN BIRDING

Green birding activities fall into three groups:

- Listing locally: Focusing on local listing challenges instead of traveling long distances to collect rare species.
- Patchworking: Regularly visiting a piece of land throughout the year, getting to know and understand the birds and other wildlife that live there.
- Conservation and citizen science: Doing your part to improve the world for birds by participating in conservation projects and submitting the data you collect to citizen science programs.

Some birders do one of these things, some another; many enjoy all three. Each represents a different side of green birding.

Listing locally

Birders love lists. Most of us keep life lists for the whole planet, and many of us have separate lists for our own region, the state or province next door, or a foreign country. It has been said in another context that "those who like that sort of thing like that sort of thing a lot" and the inveterate keeper of lists is unlikely to be cured easily of his or her obsession. After a while, the neophyte lister feels a need to compare his or her list with others and soon you find yourself birding competitively by taking part in Big Days, Big Sits, Big Years, and other contests of bird-sighting. The good news is that making a decision to limit your travel in pursuit of birds doesn't mean you have to stop birding competitively. There are green counterparts of many of the challenges I just mentioned; you'll find more details in the chapter on the sport of birding.

A bit of realism now. I understand entirely that breaking the habit of driving long distances to see birds may be a hard sell to many otherwise

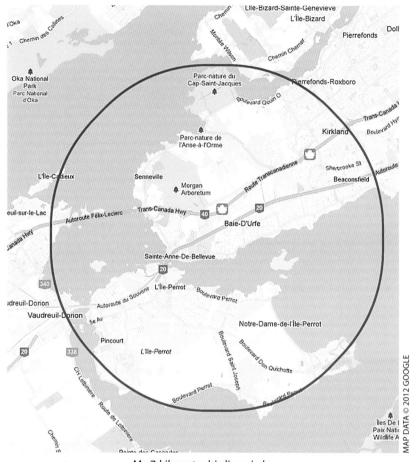

My 7-kilometer birding circle.

green-minded birders and so I have a compromise to offer. The well-known annual Audubon Christmas Bird Counts try to assess the number of birds in a circle 15 miles (24 km) in diameter. If you are not ready to commit to hardcore, entirely self-powered birding, you could establish a circle of this diameter centered on your home and try to limit your mainstream birding to what is happening within it. The circle will include your local patch, the one that you do walk or cycle to regularly, but will also put a wider range of habitats and a wider range of bird species within reach while still putting some limits on the carbon emissions produced by your birding.

For example, I have restricted myself to a circle 7 kilometers (about 4 miles) in radius that includes my personal patch and which I can get around easily under my own power. Within this circle I can find plenty of riverside habitat, an arboretum, fields, many gardens with bird-attracting shrubs and feeders, and other sites of interest. I am slightly hampered by the fact that the only ways off the island of Montreal within my self-powered reach all require, with only one inconvenient exception, the use of a car. But with a little ingenuity and plenty of pedaling or paddling, I can work around that.

I know that there are potentially between 220 and 260 species of birds that can be seen in this 7-kilometer circle at one time or another—and occasionally, some real rarities turn up. About four years ago, an Ash-throated Flycatcher spent a couple of weeks in a shrubby corner of a local park, much to my delight. This is a bird that by rights should have been down in the Caifornia/Arizona/Texas corner of the continent at that time of year, about as far away from my patch as you can be, and had obviously taken a wrong turn. Such wanderers can turn up anywhere and are to be looked out for; don't ever take small brown birds for granted!

Much of my really rich birding is centred on the Morgan Arboretum. I am rather lucky to have this so close, but it is not that different in essence from

The Pileated Woodpecker is the big bird of the forest. This one was feasting on fat grubs in a rotting log in the Morgan Arboretum, just west of Montreal and right in the center of my patch.

any reasonably extensive area of woodland, and it is quite likely that your patch will include something comparable in character, if not in size.

My other hot spot is the St. Lawrence River, which attracts rafts of water birds in migration and is home to many locally breeding species in the spring and summer months. Of course, in winter it freezes solid and the birds depart—but at the tip of the island is an area of shallow rapids under a railway bridge with a lock to allow boats to pass. Because the water is constantly in motion, this part of the river never ices over. If there are any early-moving water birds about in the first few months of the year, they will be looking for open water, and and so they tend to concentrate here. I make sure to check the spot out (it's no more than a thirty-minute walk away) regularly once the New Year is behind us. I admit that there are some better places in the region with similar characteristics, but I would have to drive to get to them. The fact that "my" open water is within walking distance, however, ensures that I check it more often than I would the more distant sites. I manage to get plenty of good water birds most winters.

In the other direction, downriver, is a large bay that is enjoyed by huge rafts of hundreds or thousands of birds such as scaup, who gather there for a couple of weeks just before freeze-up. If you spend some time carefully scanning, you will almost always find a few really desirable birds of other, rarer, species among the mass of black and white.

Those are the hot spots, but a lot of my productive birding is done while walking and cycling my suburban streets, keeping an eye on my neighbors' gardens. Even when sitting in my garden at the end of the day, I see birds passing by or flying overhead that I can make a note of. For example, as I write this part of the book it is mid-April; yesterday was a warm day so I sat on the deck for a half hour before supper and was able to see three Broad-winged Hawks pass over heading north. The first White-throated Sparrow of the spring was hopping around the grass under one of my feeders, some late-departing Dark-eyed Juncos were about still, the ever-present Common Grackles and Red-winged Blackbirds were making themsevles heard and seen, and a pair of Song Sparrows and Northern Cardinals visited my yard. There were Brown Creepers in a neighbor's trees; there were also crows, of course, and a Blue Jay screamed at me. Gulls were overhead, along with a small flight of geese. There is always something going on to make life interesting. The stars of the show, the hawks, will shortly be replaced by resident Merlins within a few minutes' walk. There are always Red-tailed, Cooper's, and Sharp-shinned Hawks around, and any day now I should see migrating Turkey Vultures, maybe a Bald Eagle or three. Up in the arboretum, the Red-shouldered Hawks will be finding a nesting site in a tall tree (they always make it hard to find—all part of the game).

Sometimes, birds just come to us. This Great Blue Heron was sunning himself on a boat in Vancouver harbor, where any urban birder could easily add it to his or her list.

Dark-eyed Juncos pass through the northern states and Canada each spring and fall, heralding the arrival of winter and its eventual demise.

My personal 7-kilometer birding circle demonstrates the excellent birding potential that you can find in almost any urban area. It is not necessary to live out in the country to find enjoyable and varied birding. As an exercise, I also drew a similar circle around the various other places where I have lived over the years to see how my birding would have been affected. These areas vary from a housing development on the outskirts of a northern industrial city in England, to semi-inner city dense housing in a major city, to a small historic town, to a village in the country, to where I live today in the leafier suburbs of Montreal. In every case, I found parks, fields, water, gardens, trees, and other places that attract and hold birds within that circle.

Your patch

Many birders, list keepers or otherwise, eventually find themselves drawn to a forest, park, marsh, or mountain near where they live; this becomes, in birders' parlance, their "patch." Birders who have decided to leave their cars behind when they go birding will spend even more time visiting and learning about their patches, an activity known as "patchworking."

You can usually find a good number of bird species in a forest. Almost any forest near your home will have excellent walking trails.

Your patch is the place you visit regularly throughout the year. You follow the same trails and peer into the same thickets season by season and soon you find that you know where the birds are before you see them. You know when they arrive in spring and leave in autumn, which birds are thriving and which are just hanging on, what they feed on, when they nest, how many broods they raise each year, and which predators like to eat them. Patchworking is the opportunity to know a small group of birds really well.

Depending on where you live, you don't even need to go far from your door to enjoy some excellent green birding. A garden designed to attract birds can draw a surprising number of species in these days when towns and agriculture are crowding out birds' habitats. Chapter 6 will explain more about how to create a bird garden.

Conservation

Sadly, in this frenetic and overpopulated world, there is more and more pressure put on the places that birds live in. Marshes are drained, forests are felled, and fields become littered with new housing or factories. As habitat is lost or fragmented, birds find it harder and harder to find a place where they can feed and raise young in safety and security. All birders should keep an eye out for potentially damaging developments, to bring them to the attention of other birders and to question their necessity, and birders who focus their activity locally are particularly well-situated to do this. Don't just bird in isolation on your patch, but join with others to protect the bird habitat that we have left to us—at the end of the day there will be more birds for us all to see and enjoy.

You can also help birds by spreading the word about green birding and encouraging other birders to change their habits. Organize a green birding contest in your area, perhaps using it to raise funds for a habitat restoration project; offer to lead self-powered birding field trips. Write a green birding blog; report your sightings on the local club's internet chat group. Give a talk to a local school or community group. And—most importantly—lead by example.

GETTING STARTED

So far, we have looked at the reasons for green birding, and we have briefly explored what serious green birding looks like. Now it's time to look at the practical details of putting this approach to birding into practice. Remember while you are trying this out that green birding is essentially about having an enjoyable and interesting time. It isn't some chore that is good for your soul, it isn't about making rules to take the fun out of birding, and it isn't compulsory. It is, however, about getting to know your local area and its wildlife better—and it is surprisingly addictive for many of us.

What works for you?

First of all, this is not an all-or-nothing commitment for life. Take it out for a test run first and see just how far you feel able and willing to change your habits. Do that and then do your best to stick to your plans. Naturally, I would like to encourage everyone to become a totally green birder, but I am a realist—and I'm also still susceptible, as are we all, to the call of that "occasional" rarity in the next county. There are going to be occasions when the chance of the sighting of a lifetime is simply too strong to resist, and that's fine. We each do what we can and all our small contributions, added together, become meaningful.

Nevertheless, having decided to significantly reduce your carbon footprint while in pursuit of good birds, you first need to decide what is practical in your personal circumstances. Are you only going to bird in areas you can reach on foot or by bike? Will you use public transportation? Will you confine yourself to a Christmas Bird Count–style 15-mile circle? Frankly, green birding is a lot simpler and easier to stick to you if your home happens to be surrounded by trees and fields and streams than if you live in a city-center condominium with concrete and busy streets as far as the eye can see—though if you are in the latter category, well, that's what scheduled public transportation is for.

Going for a walk

Now, let's get started. Put on some boots, grab your binoculars and a notebook, and step outside your door. Start walking and look about you.

Lots of houses have bird feeders these days, even if they aren't regularly kept topped up with food. It's a good idea to check them. You might get strange looks from neighbors wondering why you are staring at their gardens, but my experience is that as long as you are obviously looking at the birds on the feeders and not staring through their windows, most people are pleased that you are enjoying their birds too. What's more, they are almost always happy to have your help identifying some bird they see often but don't know the name of, so don't be too shy about what you are doing.

As you continue your walk, look around your neighborhood for places where birds like to hang out. Scan parks and empty lots; look for perching flycatchers in the trees and swallows over a bit of swampy ground. Make a note of what you have seen. The purpose of this exploratory expedition is really to familiarize yourself with the neighborhood. Try to think like a bird and look at your locale as it probably appears to the birds. You want to get a good feel for what's around you because as you continue your local walk in search of birds, you will want to work out the most productive routes to take.

Of course, birding this way is something you can do whenever you go out. Taking the dog for a walk? Don't forget the binoculars. Going to the

If your birding patch is in the Southwest, there is a good chance it holds Gilded Flickers like this one, seen just outside Tuscon, Arizona.

store for a carton of milk? Binoculars, please! Romantic stroll in the gloaming with your partner? Maybe smaller compact binoculars in your pocket this time—just keep your eyes and ears open all the time as you get to know your neighborhood better.

The next stage is to repeat this process, but this time do it on a bicycle. Your morning birding walk might have taken you three miles, but your bike is good for ten or fifteen in the same time, and you will undoubtedly find a lot more possible bird-holding areas that you will want to keep an eye on.

Is there a stream or lake near your home? Hook your canoe onto a pair of transport wheels and tow it behind your bike. Launch it on the water and start creeping up on those ducks and shorebirds.

You can repeat this process from your place of work. You have to travel there every day anyway, and you probably spend as much time there each day as you do at home; it is an entirely legitimate second place on which to center your green birding activities. Plus, we all know that a lunchtime walk is good for body and soul—and so a lunchtime walk with birds thrown in must be even better.

As you venture out, keep some simple records of the birds that you are seeing: species, numbers, habitat, and so on. Seasoned birders will be doing this anyway, but newcomers might need a little help in the best way to go about it. In the next chapter, we'll look at recording and reporting birds in some detail, but for now just put a notebook and pencil in your pocket and try to develop a system for writing things down. You are trying to build up a picture of your local birds over the course of the changing seasons.

Picking your spot

Now that you have a good idea of what is within reach of a short expedition from home, you might want to decide what your local "patch" is going to be. If you have been birding for a while you probably already have a favorite local spot that you visit with some regularity; green birding moves this concept to a higher level of intensity. Among the various places that you have been checking out in your walks and bike rides, is there an area of woodland, a field, a stream, a lake, or a park that seems to have good birding opportunities and (this is important) that you enjoy visiting? We all have somewhere we like to go strolling, even when not actively birding, and that is the sort of place that you should look for when selecting a patch. And don't overlook

Birders scan the shoreline for rarities. Whenever birds congregate, pause and look them over carefully—there may be a rarity mixed in among the common birds.

the fact that even in very familiar territory there may be birdy corners that you don't know about. You can use web-based mapping and satellite imaging tools like Google Earth to help you search them out.

Get connected

Although there are innumerable books and websites devoted to birds and birding and plenty of people who like to do their birding alone, when it comes to improving your skills and birding know-how nothing quite surpasses meeting and learning from experienced birders, or just birders with a different experience from yours. Birders are (*almost* always) sociable and friendly people who are happy to discuss sightings and share insights and knowledge when we meet up in the field. Probably the best way to tap into this resource and make new birding friends is by joining a local birding club. These organizations, of which there are thousands, vary from small groups of birders living in a particular town and meeting on a fairly social basis to regional and national clubs and societies, many of which often have a charitable arm to their activities as well as a more educational and social side of things.

You can also connect to other birders online. There are several websites, blogs, and forums on the internet that are managed by green birders who are

Go out on local bird club outings and learn from expert leaders. However well you think you know your local area, there is always someone who knows something you don't.

keen to spread the word about the movement or to share their experiences. A Google search will turn up plenty in short order (try terms like "green birding," and "bigby"). Make sure to visit www.greenbirding.ca, the first site to promote this alternative form of birding and the place where the term "Bigby" (an abbreviation of Big Green Big Year) first emerged. You can register with this site (free) and join the green birding–focused forums there; this is a great way to connect with other birders who are interested in changing the way we pursue our hobby.

"After I reported the find [of a rare bird in the area]. . . I expected some birders to drive to the area to see this rare bird, but I confess that I was really surprised to see how many people came, and surprised that people would drive so far on the chance that they might see one individual bird which could take off at any time. Birders came from all corners of Connecticut, of course, but I saw a Massachusetts license plate among the many, many cars that streamed through the little cemetery during the week, and I know of at least one person who came all the way from New York.

"On one of my stops there, I chatted briefly with two birders from the southwestern corner of the state who had driven 60 and 70 miles, respectively, on the chance that they might see the bird.

"'Oh, this is great,' the woman said happily. 'Now I can check this off on my state list.'

"She didn't say a word about the bird. Nothing like 'I've never seen anything like that slaty-blue plumage,' or 'Isn't it amazing that it can dive and feed in that turbulent water?' or 'I wonder how it ended up here?'

"Her very next comment to me was, 'seen any Rusty Blackbirds?' She drove for two hours in rush hour traffic to tick the bird on her list, and that was it; I watched her pack up and drive away to look for the next bird on her list."

—Sarah Hagar Johnston,
http://quodlibet-sarah.blogspot.com

Patchworking

3

arlier in this book we looked into selecting your own birding patch—a place within easy self-powered access of your home where you can go "patchworking," observing in depth the birds there over the year. Time now to look briefly at what your patch is and how you can best enjoy the birding you find there.

Your patch is that piece of land, however large or small, that you visit regularly throughout the year While there, you keep an eye out for new and interesting species, noting migration arrivals and departures and simply enjoying being with your birds. Most patchworkers will keep a list of the birds they have seen on their patch—often both a life patch list and an annual patch list so they can compare season to season and year to year and be aware of changes.

As a green birder, of course, you need to pick a place that you can easily reach by foot or by cycle or on a bus (or it could be an island that you reach by canoe—that would be rather exceptional, but very desirable). Of course, it would be nice if we could all have birding patches that are wild and beautiful and full of the rarest of birds, but realistically you probably live in a city or suburb and that can limit your choices. Accessibility, even in bad weather, is paramount for the patchworking birder. Naturally, you will also want your chosen patch to be a pleasant place so that visiting it is always a pleasure rather than a chore.

So, what should you look for in a "good" patch? First, it has to appeal to you and be close enough to your home base to make it not too onerous for you to visit it fairly regularly. It has to be somewhere that you take pleasure in walking or cycling to. Only after that does it have to be perfect for birds. I know that might sound like a strange thing to say—but birds are remarkably adaptive, and there are not many places that do not attract a good variety of species.

Do you have any marshland near your home? All those mosquitoes bring in the birds like nothing else does.

Of course, some sites are more effective than others. Look for a varied environment: some open grassy areas that are not regularly cut (grazing land is excellent, but so is a school playing field if it has some bushy areas round the edges), some shrubby spots, and an area of mature trees perhaps. If it has water—a pool or a stream—then you are well on your way to having a very bird-rich patch indeed. If you live in a rural area this list will probably not be hard to fulfill, but even in dense urban places it is remarkable how often a small stream with unkempt banks and shrubs will snake its way between housing developments into the heart of a city. These tracts of land are often highways for wildlife that use them to penetrate the urban jungle in search of food.

Your patch doesn't have to be some wild and exotic spot. Any spot where birds can be found will do. Your garden, the neighborhood park, an urban green space, a cemetery or churchyard, a forest or marsh, a school yard, an abandoned railway cutting, or a sewage farm would all make interesting patches. A number of birders do their patchworking in the streets around their homes, checking up on the urban birds and visitors to neighbors'

Moving water, whether in the forest or in your garden, is a magnet for birds.

feeders, with the addition of the occasional patch of scrub—a corner of a park or the bushes along a railway track—to add variety. However built up your area may be, there are almost always places that birds can make a living in. And if the birds are there, the birder can enjoy them. I am lucky to live near a large university-owned arboretum with extensive trails that I have adopted as my patch. However, idyllic as it sounds, because it is attractive it is also full of people taking exercise and consequently the birds, although very plentiful, can be shy and hard to find at times. On the other hand, one of my friends has chosen as his patch an old, worked-out sand quarry with a bit of water at the bottom. It seems almost barren by comparison but in fact is famous in the area for the richness and variety of birds because it is relatively undisturbed by people and their dogs.

There is nothing to stop you from picking your garden as your patch. Indeed, some amazingly rich birding can be enjoyed in a well-designed garden. I'll explain more about how to make your garden a center of green birding activity in chapter 6.

Of course, you are not going to see hundreds of terrifically interesting and rare birds on your first visit to your patch, but as you continue to bird there you will gradually get to know where to find the local birds. You will soon start to identify that quiet corner that is reliable for Song Thrushes and the reedy section of stream that's home to an elusive Virginia Rail. You'll happen across a nest of robins or kestrels and then watch, carefully and discretely, as the eggs hatch and the young fledge and fly away—and the next year you'll be looking out for the adults to return and start building a new nest. On your patch you don't just tick or even count the birds but you actively watch, study, and enjoy what they are doing. You will take time to go slowly and become involved in their lives.

You'll begin to see lots of things that you would miss in a place you only visit very occasionally. You'll find yourself starting to notice which trees develop their spring leaves first and which let them fall first at the end of summer. You will discover where certain species of birds like to take shelter on bright, cool May mornings, while they wait for the temperature-dependent insects they eat to start appearing. You will notice which migratory birds appear first in the spring and where they are most likely to be found. Gradually, quite unconsciously, you will begin to understand the patterns of life on your patch and even start to look for events before they happen. You will go out and expect to see a particular bird or flower simply because that's what was there this time last year and the year before.

After two or three seasons of regular visits, you will begin to notice changes in the populations as different seasonal visitors arrive in the springtime and depart in the fall. The exciting bit is when you begin to recognize and even anticipate the common birds on your patch with ease or, better

The American Crow is an ubiquitous bird that everyone should have somewhere on their patch. It's a very handy bird, too, when you are trying to find owls or hawks.

still, without even realizing that you are doing it. Because you are the regular birder on your patch and may visit it fifty or a hundred times a year you will often find that you are the first person on the scene when a good bird shows up, one that other birders will also want to see. Don't forget that you see these good birds not only because you are expecting them but also because you are there looking for them.

As you work your patch you'll likely start keeping records of your observations over the seasons and over the years. If you are really into your patch you will probably add additional information to your notes on the species and numbers of birds you see; you may note weather patterns, particular foliage features, and the presence or absence of food sources. Gradually the picture will develop.

Your records will help you to see trends and notice changes that you would otherwise have missed. These could be simple things such as comparing the number of bird species seen on your patch from year to year, or they can be more detailed. For example, I noted the presence on my patch of a Red-bellied Woodpecker (a really exciting bird in my area, as they are not "supposed" to be this far north) four years in a row. Some of your observations will be of interest to other birders, and you can start to share the materials

The mewing call of this Gray Catbird had me crawling through thorny undergrowth to find him, but he had the decency to sit still in the sunshine, giving me a good soul-satisfying view, once he was tracked down.

you have gathered. You may find that you become the expert on your patch, the person that people will seek out first when planning a trip to your area.

Once you start to really get to know a patch of ground really intimately, to the extent that you notice all the little changes every time you visit it, you start to realize that you and that bit of land have a deep connection and you will want to nurture the relationship and deepen your knowledge even further. You'll start asking questions about your patch. Are the numbers of birds there rising or falling? Did the swallows return in spring early or late this year, and when they arrived were there adequate populations of insects for them to raise their young? A new housing development has been built nearby—is it affecting the birdlife on your patch? The spring was late and cold; what effect has that had? Why are you suddenly not seeing any birds of a particular species?

I could go on but I think the best way to show you how important and enjoyable local patch birding can be is to offer you a quotation from someone who is already patch birding and having a great time at it. Scott Cronenweth is a Maine birder who patchworks a semi-urban park. He blogs at www.eons.com/blogs/blog/ScottCronenweth.

However you approach it, birding regularly on your patch adds depth, fulfillment, and fun to your birding.

So—where is your patch going to be?

Birding Your Patch

Birding your patch is a wonderful way to become intimate with the Earth, to learn what birds to expect and when to expect them, and perhaps even to make a contribution to conservation or science. Really getting to know a patch also greatly increases the chances that you'll notice unexpected or unusual birds that you'll be excited to share with your friends or even report on your local "rare bird alert" hotline.

[My patch] is far from a pristine environment but, in a largely developed matrix of waterfront industry and house lots, it's an oasis for migrating birds in spring and fall and also provides acceptable breeding and wintering habitat for some birds of the forest edge. In fact, Hinckley Park is very popular with local birders in spring, who come looking for migrant warblers, orioles, sparrows, swallows, and other so-called "passerines" or "perching birds." And because it's a good spot for migrants it's also a good spot, at times, for migrating raptors interested in a moveable feathered feast.

British twitchers call the good birds they find on their patches "patch-ticks." Fun patch-ticks for me at Hinckley Park include Worm-eating Warbler, Canada Warbler, a "fallout" of hundreds of warblers and vireos (including several Philadelphias and a Yellow-throated) one drizzly May morning, Wood Duck, Common Merganser, Peregrine Falcon, Osprey, Merlin, Barred Owl, Solitary Sandpiper, Scarlet Tanager, White-crowned Sparrow, White-eyed Vireo (a great bird for Maine), and many others. Recently I even saw a beaver there, resting on the ice of the upper pond.

—Scott Cronenweth

White-crowned Sparrow

"Last year I began a quest to get in shape and have fun birding by keeping a list of species I saw while biking or walking from my back door. . . Last year I tallied 192 species by non-motorized transport (NMT) and biked 1374 kilometers; my goals this year (2011) were to find 200 species and bike over 2000 kilometers.

"By the end of May I had 170 species, but then things got tough. I added a few species over the summer—a Flammulated Owl in a nest-box a few kilometers from home, a Black Swift rocketing over the house, a female Gray Partridge with a youngster walking across the lawn. Fall migration brought a few shorebird species, but Penticton has few mudflats so I've missed a number of species that would have been easy farther north in the Okanagan Valley.

"This kind of birding isn't always easy. On September 19th I set off to Kaleden to look for a Red-breasted Sapsucker reported a couple of days previously. After pedalling for 20 kilometers and climbing a big hill, I was just pulling into the driveway to look for the sapsucker when my phone rang. It was a friend breathlessly reporting a Sabine's Gull back in Penticton, only minutes away from my house. Agh! Needless to say, I looked in vain for the sapsucker for 40 minutes, managing only to call in a Northern Pygmy-Owl. Disappointed, I biked back to Penticton but couldn't find any trace of the gull. Strike two.

"There are a good number of possible species I can add to my year's list over the next two months—perhaps a Greater White-fronted Goose will appear on the golf course with the Canadas, or a Harlequin Duck might show up at Okanagan Falls. I haven't seen a Northern Goshawk or Rough-legged Hawk yet, both reasonably common wintering birds around here. And maybe I'll finally have to make that hike up the mountain to get Dusky Grouse, Gray Jay, and Pine Grosbeak. All I need is a half-dozen species—and I'm only 181 kilometers shy of the 2000 mark!"

—Dick Cannings, http://dickcannings.com

Equipment and Record-Keeping

4

I t's a fair assumption that if you are reading this book, you already have all the basic things you need to be a birder: if you have a pair of binoculars, a notebook, and the ability to walk, that's about it. However, as with most activities, there is some additional equipment that can make your birding a bit more comfortable and enjoyable. In addition, green birding presents an extra equipment challenge: without the convenience of a car, you have to transport everything you need on your own back (or bike). In this chapter I will introduce to you some useful "kit" that you may want to consider and offer some handy tips for transporting equipment on a lengthy birding day from my own experience.

EQUIPMENT FOR SELF-POWERED BIRDING
Walking
Binoculars, of course, are the most important tool for all birders. As a walking birder, you don't have any extra considerations beyond the basic rule of binocular selection: buy the best you can. If there is any single thing on earth that exemplifies the "you get what you pay for" concept, then it is your choice of optics. Almost without exception, cheap optics are deficient optics in one way or another. Plenty of other books, websites, and specialist dealers will advise you on the best choice for your budget—but quite likely you made this decision long ago. You may want to get a different carrying device for your binoculars, however, since you are going to be walking a long way with them. If your glass makes your neck ache after a couple of hours, consider using a shoulder harness rather than a neck strap or, if the weather allows it, keep them in the capacious pocket of a good jacket. So long as you can get at them quickly this works well.

We don't always happen to be actively birding when that special bird pops its head up. Maybe you are walking your dog or on the way to the store when

Lightweight optics make the walking easier. You can get huge, heavy scopes, but the walking birder might prefer optics that are a little lighter and easier to carry. Smaller doesn't always have to mean lower quality.

you chance upon it. Being prepared is important and I would suggest that you think about investing in a second pair of small, pocket-sized binoculars. These will take up hardly any room and are light enough that you can always have them with you. Make them part of your triple-check before you leave home every day: keys, wallet or purse, and binoculars. Some of these pocket binoculars are amazingly good quality and weigh almost nothing—and on the day you need them, you'll be *really* glad you invested in them.

The clothing you'll wear depends on the weather, but because you won't have a car to leave things in until you need them, you might choose a jacket with large pockets so that you can at least have a notebook, camera, and field guide readily available. You may decide to bring a light backpack or a small messenger bag so you can also take along a waterproof jacket and a water bottle.

Depending on the territory you are surveying and the likelihood of seeing birds at a distance, you may wish to take your spotting scope along for the day. You could regret it if you don't. The trouble with spotting scopes, of course, is that they are bulky and heavy. There are many solutions that supposedly make the carrying more comfortable but only one really does the job.

The cheapest and simplest means of carrying your scope and tripod are to put it all on your shoulder; unfortunately it won't be long before things start to ache and the rest of your day will be so uncomfortable that you may well leave the scope at home next time and miss a lifer. Many birders purchase pads for the tripod legs or, less expensively, make their own from foam pipe insulation bought at the hardware store. This is certainly much more comfortable, but even so, after a day in the field your shoulder is going to ache. The other downside to carrying your scope over your shoulder is that you need one hand to steady it; if you suddenly need to get those binoculars onto a bird you are going to be hampered. I have missed several excellent views of birds because it took too much time to put the tripod down and get my second hand free.

Option two for the tripod and scope problem is one of the several harnesses that are made specifically for this purpose. They usually allow the scope to be carried on your back like a backpack and are many times more comfortable than carrying it over your shoulder. Both your hands are free for the binoculars at all times. These harnesses are an excellent alternative, but they do have their drawbacks. First, you have to choose between scope harness and

Every birder needs good binoculars.

Left: Carrying a tripod the "traditional" way—simple, but hard on the shoulders. Right: An efficient tripod harness will reduce strain on your back and shoulders while keeping your equipment accessible.

backpack, as you only have one back and pair of shoulders; secondly, if you need to get that scope set up quickly you will waste minutes doing so.

There is at least one specialist backpack (the "Scopesack") made for photographers who have long lenses mounted on their tripods. In essence this is a padded, tubular backpack with outer pockets and no top. All you have to do is to upend your scope and tripod over your head and drop them, scope end down, into the tube. You can use the outer pockets to carry small items such as your lunch and your field guide. This setup is rather bulky but surprisingly effective and comfortable for a long day. You can even leave the legs extended in open country where there are no low branches, allowing you quick access to the scope. It is a bit of a problem when it rains but that's easily fixed with a large plastic bag.

By far the best carrying method that I have found for the walking green birder in need of a scope at some point during the day is a harness that was designed and made by Centre de Conservation de la Faune Ailée/Nature Expert, a specialist birding store in Montreal (www.ccfa-montreal.com) and available by mail-order. This simple and elegant solution consists of a heavy-duty bandolier-style strap worn diagonally over one shoulder with an attached waist-belt for stability. The scope hangs by your side from this by a quick-release buckle that can be operated with one hand. The design and materials

A specialized backpack for carrying a tripod and scope.

are based on long-tested military and police equipment, and it is amazingly comfortable—you will barely know you are carrying a scope, so well is the weight distributed. It can be worn under or over a jacket, leaves both hands free, and allows you to carry a backpack as well. This is definitely the best solution for the green birder who has a long way to walk. And the single-hand release is a great feature when that neighborhood dog or a startled bear starts eyeing up your legs . . . nothing like a stout tripod to fend off critters!

If you are also a photographer and want to take a camera that is larger than a pocket point-and-shoot with you then you are going to have to choose between practicality and instant readiness to capture that shot of a lifetime. In general, hanging both binoculars and a camera around your neck can be awkward; it is certainly heavy and may result in something getting banged harder than you would like as the day progresses. In general, as a birder you are probably more concerned with the birds than with photographs of birds and so keeping the camera in your backpack is perhaps the wisest counsel I can offer. Having said that, I confess that I more often than is sensible walk about with both pieces of equipment hanging off me.

The answer to this dilemma may lie with the photography equipment companies rather than the birding ones. There are harness systems designed for professional (often press) photographers that allow for multiple cameras

Know your birding territory! There are some species of wildlife you may not want to meet on foot, so be sure you're prepared.

to be quickly available. Usually these can be simply adapted so that instead of two cameras you carry one plus your binoculars. Not only do these systems answer the accessibility conundrum, they also distribute the not inconsiderable weight remarkably well so that you don't get "birders' neck" after an hour or so tramping the trails of your local patch.

Biking

Your choice of bicycle is fairly simple—you'll want either a mountain bike or a hybrid bike, with a comfortable seat and broad tires. Sit-up-and-beg handlebars are best because if you're biking with your head low while you grip dropped handles, you're going to miss a lot of birds. Look up and look around.

Getting about by bike greatly increases the territory that you can cover and so increases the likelihood of adding additional birds to your lists, but it also brings up the question of how to safely pack and carry your equipment so that it is not susceptible to damage but is still easily available when needed.

Your binoculars will, of course, be around your neck at all times, but if you're biking with them you should seriously consider hanging them from a chest harness instead of a neck strap. The last thing you want as you make that rapid course correction in traffic is a heavy piece of glass and metal swinging about to distract you.

You won't need to rapidly access your scope and tripod, but they are expensive pieces of equipment and you will want to secure them in a manner which maximizes their safety. You can buy a special container for carrying your folded tripod on a bike—but in essence it is not much more than an expensive nylon tube with straps to tighten it that allows you to carry the tripod horizontally along the rear pannier frame of your bike. It is not difficult to make up something similar for yourself, using either bungee cords or quick-release nylon straps to hold it in place. My suggestion is that you get a really solid all-purpose rear rack for your bike, available from any good bicycle store. These are designed to carry all sorts of odd-shaped and awkward equipment, and you should be able to come up with a system that suits your particular bike and the size and weight of your tripod.

In the section on walking, we discussed systems for strapping your tripod and scope on your back. When cycling this may be a good option, especially since you can carry your other things in a conventional bike pannier, but a word of caution: even the lightest scope and tripod combination is not all that light and having it on your back raises your center of gravity, increasing your instability.

Convenient or not, you may want to find a way to carry the equipment fairly low down, for safety's sake. Think about getting two panniers—one for your coat, lunch, books, and so on, and one for your tripod and scope. In my opinion, this is the best compromise. You can also get specially padded and sectioned pannier bags for carrying photography gear on a bike.

Traveling on the water

There are several options here, but more than likely the boating birder will be traveling by canoe or kayak. Rowing boats are wonderfully stable for birding but hard work, and as for punts, well, you have to be British to understand the superiority of a punt in shallow waters—and to know how to handle one. But a canoe or kayak is an excellent choice. Most water and shorebirds seem to expect threats to approach them from land and take little notice of a gently paddled canoe creeping up on them, thus allowing you excellent close-up views.

The important thing to remember is that optics and cameras need to be kept dry—and they will sink like a stone if dropped in the water. Keep all your equipment other than the essential binoculars in a waterproof container when not in use (you can get suitable containers at stores that sell boating equipment) and have it all well secured in the boat so that it cannot fall out.

Take special care when actually watching birds from your craft. It is all too easy to make a sudden turn or movement that can upend your kayak or canoe. You know the situation—a star bird flies across the water and you,

Birders don't often thank dogs for being around, but the one that spooked this Mallard made the shot.

Canoes are a very green—and peaceful—way to find birds.

binoculars fixed to your eyes, turn to follow it . . . and *splash,* your boat rolls and you are in the water. Maybe this shouldn't happen, but it does, simply because having your gaze directed through the binoculars or camera eyepiece distances your brain from the realities of what you are doing. Even the most experienced boater can fall prey to this disaster in waiting. Move slowly and be aware of your body at all times.

Don't be put off by the fact that you don't live on the river or lakeshore. Using your own human power to get your canoe to the nearest water is not that hard. You can buy, for a modest sum, a pair of wheels mounted on a special frame that you can strap your canoe or kayak to from any canoe store. Usually, these are designed to allow you to walk while hauling the boat along with one hand, and they work very well. You can attach it to your bike with a short cord or piece of webbing from the carry handle at the front or rear of your canoe. This is a very easy way to transport your canoe considerable distances . . . although I don't think you should try taking it along major highways by this means.

Skiing and snowshoeing

Birding in the winter is hugely rewarding. I live in southern Quebec, where we have truly cold and snow-filled winters, yet even so the annual Christmas

Snowshoes are a good means of self-powered birding in winter. If you are struggling to make your way through the snow you will reduce your chance of seeing birds—so properly prepare for the current weather conditions.

Bird Count can find in the region of 80 to 100 species most years. The resident species that never migrate are supplemented by more northerly birds coming south for easier food—and this principle applies almost anywhere from the states along the Canadian border and northwards. Mega-birds like Snowy Owls and Great Gray Owls are probably only going to be seen by most of us when the world is white.

The "owling season" is a great compensation to birders for the cold of winter. There are most certainly more owls on your patch than you suspect. This one is a Northern Saw-whet Owl.

If you are a skier or snowshoe aficionado you already know about keeping warm and how to move in snow. And unless you know there is going to be a bird worth the effort, you probably will not want to take the scope and tripod with you. Thus the only special things the winter green birder requires are binoculars and a notebook.

You will be surprised, though, what you can see. Even walking along the snowy streets of a city suburb can turn up unexpectedly exciting bird species attracted by the shelter offered by houses and hedges and the food put out on feeders. Winter is, above all, the time for checking your neighbors' gardens and compost heaps.

RECORDING YOUR BIRD SIGHTINGS

There is very little about the process of recording that is exclusive to green birding. Nevertheless, keeping good, meticulous records is so fundamental that it is worth discussing here as a core feature of the green birder's activities.

We record the birds we see for a multitude of reasons. Most birders keep personal life lists; for this purpose simply jotting names of species and perhaps numbers of individual birds in a notebook is all that is necessary. A part of green birding, however, is conservation—and conservation cannot be effective without detailed, accurate knowledge of the habitats being investigated and the birds and other creatures that make use of them. As a birder who focuses his or her efforts locally, you are uniquely placed to provide the in-depth observations conservationists and citizen science projects need. In chapter 8 we will discuss ways you can contribute the data you collect to various citizen science projects, but for now we will concentrate on the "how" of record-keeping.

What should you record?

All birders out in the field are potential scientists. Ornithology, out of all the field sciences, has benefited most from the huge amounts of data gathered by ordinary people just like you over the years. Indeed, many important facts about birdlife would never have been known had it not been for keen and observant amateurs and their notebooks. But for our observations to be valuable it is essential that we collect our data in a consistent and effective way, so that we can compare the information we gather over the months and years and extract meaningful conclusions.

Scientists talk about having a "data collection protocol," and this is a concept that applies to amateur birders as well. A data collection protocol just means that you decide what you will record and then you make sure that you always collect that information—and record it in the same way every time. Whether you record a little or a lot of material about each sighting matters less than having consistent records.

Each time you go birding—in fact, each time that you see a bird, whatever else you are doing at the time—you should make sure to note at least the species you saw, the date, the time of day, and the location. Without date, time, and place anything else you write down is going to be of diminished value.

The next "layer" of information includes such things as whether you were birding alone or in a group (and how many were in the group), the weather, the distance you walked or biked, the start and end times of your birding session, and a brief description of the type of habitat where you saw the bird. If the bird is a new one for your life list, it is worthwhile to estimate the number you saw and note whether you actually saw the birds in question or identified them by sound. Some of this data, such as the distance traveled and the number of people in your party, may seem of minor importance, but in fact they are significant as they are measures of "effort" and help those who analyze your data to more accurately extrapolate local bird populations from your reports. For example, it is improbable that you will have seen all the Blue Jays in an area, but if you have seen some, then statistical techniques can estimate how many others there were that you didn't see—and the number of people who were looking for birds affects that calculation.

For those who find this stuff interesting, there is quite a lot more that we can record that is going to be useful. Were the birds male or female, adults or juveniles? Were they engaged in activities that indicate they were breeding nearby or do you think they were just resting or foraging for food or fighting over territory? Did they sing? Did they utter alarm calls? What interactions between individual birds did you observe? Was the weather affecting their behavior? Did they seem to be healthy and in good condition? Once you start to note these things the list becomes almost endless, and you find yourself recording more and more each time you go out.

These kinds of observations are vitally important and nothing is too trivial to make a note of. Take, for example the humble House Sparrow. For centuries this species has been part of the background for birders, a "trash" bird to many who barely bother to notice it except to denigrate it as a foreign interloper that competes with native American birds for nesting cavities. But a few years ago, birders suddenly realized that the sparrows were not all that common any longer. In fact, their numbers were in serious and inexplicable decline. Had population statistics been kept earlier then this decline might have been spotted sooner, but because of their ubiquity we were all blind to the important changes in their numbers. Studying common birds and trying to keep common birds common benefits all bird species. The green birder is an essential link in the data collection chain that ensures that we can identify changes and take action before it is too late.

Electronic records to augment your notebook

The simplest and most comprehensive means of note-taking is still the good old notebook and pencil (a pencil rather than a pen because it is not affected by rain on the paper). All birders should have these two basics in their pockets whenever they are out in the field—you just never know when there might be something worth jotting down! Notebooks are also best for sketches. However, there are a number of electronic record-keeping options available to us today that can save you time and reduce transcription errors when you transfer your data to an online database. If you have a smartphone, you may want to give some of these options a try.

A number of easy-to-use birding database apps allow you to record the birds that you have seen with just a couple of touches on the screen—for the most part, a lot faster than the notebook. At the moment most of these are available for the iPhone but they are becoming more common on Android smartphones as well. At least one of these apps (by the time this book is published there may be others) goes even further. "Birdwatcher," released by Stevens Creek Software and available from the iPhone App Store, records your GPS coordinates when you enter a bird sighting so that when you return home you can print out a map of your walking or biking route with

 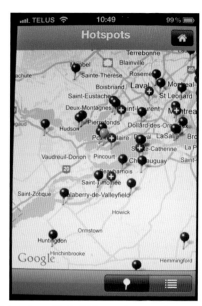

Left: You can use apps to record your bird sightings. Right: This app lets you know the best local hotspots and where rare birds have been sighted in your area.

the location of every bird you saw clearly marked. It also works in conjunction with Google maps. This is very useful if you want to direct other birders to a particular rarity; it is also rather nice to have for your records.

An alternative, albeit a less user-friendly one, to the iPhone app that records the exact place where you sighted a bird is to carry a mapping-enabled GPS such as the Garmin CX unit. These can be loaded with topographic maps and will record your track as you walk or cycle about your patch looking for birds. With one of these you will be able to flag specific spots where something of interest happened. These devices have advantages and disadvantages. On the one hand, their mapping ability is superior to that of the iPhone—especially if you are in the backwoods and without cell-phone signal—but on the other hand, you will need to have your notebook on hand to record that track-mark 47 was a Lincoln's Sparrow and that track-mark 48 was the hawk that ate it. These mapping GPS units are not anything like the more limited route-finding ones you have in your car; they have much better signal reception and tighter location-finding capability. In an emergency they will also help you to find your way home when you get lost in the woods.

But we can do more and we can do it easily. In addition to the note-taking apps and those for recording your sightings, there are an ever-growing number of excellent electronic field guides (many of them being much fuller-featured and more portable than printed guides), collections of searchable bird songs,

The compactness of electronic field guide apps is great for the walking birder—less to carry!

A mapping-style GPS unit.

and other specialist tools. You can use these apps to run through a collection of songs to help you identify an elusive call heard in the forest, compare complex field marks with ease, and read information about habitat preferences and migration routes—and all of it in a much more compact format than the old-fashioned printed field guide. This is especially great for birders who, for example, like using the Sibley guide for the illustrations, the Peterson for details of field marks, and the National Geographic for species descriptions. With smartphone apps you can have them all available in your pocket.

Photographic birding records

We have discussed the relative merits of paper and pocket computer for recording birding information—but images are sometimes the best note-taking devices of all. This book is not about bird photography—the world has enough of them already. I do, though, want to encourage you to carry a small camera with you in the field. Unless you are a serious photographer, you don't have to carry a high-end DSLR and tripod wherever you go birding, but a cell-phone camera or a decent pocket point-and-shoot digital camera is light and easy to carry and use. And having a picture of the bird you saw can make all the difference when you need to ask for help with an identification or prove to your local records committee that you did indeed see a Snow

Bunting in Florida (unlikely) or an Ash-throated Flycatcher in Quebec (it has happened). As a non-driving birder you want to travel light, but modern compact cameras take excellent pictures and are easy to carry with you in a backpack, pocket, or belt pouch.

I think that it is worthwhile getting into the habit of taking quick record shots—even if the bird's image is small and a bit fuzzy, doing so is excellent practice. It isn't simply a question of photographing the birds to get something worthy of framing and hanging on your wall. A record of the habitat you saw a bird in is also very useful, especially if you saw the bird somewhere you would not normally expect it to be. Ultimately, that record photo might make all the difference between being acknowledged as the person who saw the first species-X in your area and being laughed out of town as the amateur who couldn't tell a common Y from a rare and desirable Z. Even if they'll never be in *National Geographic*, those pictures may save your reputation.

Listing software

So we have recorded the minutest details of the birds we have seen, we have dashed off a few record shots on our compact cameras, and maybe we've even captured the GPS coordinates of all the birds we have walked or cycled or canoed past. Now that we are home again at the end of the day, what do we do next?

The next step is to take those notes and collate them in some manner that will allow you to keep track of your sightings over the years. This is where computers and the internet come into play.

I suggest that you consider purchasing a specialized bird-listing database program and using it to keep track of all your sightings. There are such programs on the market for Windows computers, and some for Mac OSX computers as well, but they all do pretty much the same job; which one you choose depends on how you like to work and how much you want to spend on the software. As long as the program you get has a simple system for entering records and an equally simple method of getting them out again, you will be well set up. Some of the options have the ability to add text notes to sightings and upload photographs, features which are very handy to have. Do a web search and ask other birders what they like. My personal recommendations from experience with several software packages would be AviSys for the Windows computer and Bird Brain for the Mac—but shop around, because your preferences may be different from mine.

These birding databases all come preloaded with regional and world lists of birds, and many will allow you to produce site-specific checklists to narrow the selection for particular places you visit. In addition to recording your life list, they can automatically produce the popular sub-lists for state, town, garden, and so on that so many birders like to keep. Some of the more recent

Recording sightings on the computer at the end of the day.

Your computer can compile your life list for you.

programs will also help you to automatically upload your sightings to an online database such as eBird. In fact, you could use eBird as your sole listing method. It is easy to use, and it is also free.

Any of these tools will make your birding life easier and more fun and help you look back in years to come and recall great days in the field. I think you will agree that it is much easier to find out when you saw your first Whimbrel by means of a couple of keystrokes than it is to hunt though a shelf full of old and curling notebooks.

Reporting to the wider world

Now that we have put our personal bird lists and observations in order, it is time to use that information to help the real science of birds. Citizen scientists have helped create the knowledge we have about birds and bird behavior for generations, perhaps more than for any other biological field, and green birders are an important link in that tradition.

The single most important place to send your sightings is the immense international birding database maintained by the scientists of the Cornell Laboratory of Ornithology in New York state at www.ebird.org

eBird is an online database of bird sightings submitted by birders all over the world; its goal is to gather as much data as possible together into one place where it will be available to scientists, educators, land managers, and conservation biologists. The database was created by the Cornell University Laboratory of Ornithology, through whom you access it in the US; access in Canada is managed via Bird Studies Canada. Much of the data that is submitted to eBird is provided by traditional birders and will often be in the form of one-off sets of observations made on a particular day at a particular site. To create a year-round picture of birdlife at that site, therefore, the eBird database relies on many more birders happening by and adding their own one-off day lists. Over time, of course, that does happen and a picture of the site is built up in considerable detail. However, the eBird people are especially interested in receiving regular reports from patch birders who visit their sites frequently and know them in depth—in fact, they have set up a special part of the online entry pages to capture just this information. Once you have set up a location at eBird you don't have to go through the full process again, just select your patch's name from a list. Green birders like us are, of course, exactly the sort of birders who are most likely to be able to collect and report this kind of regular, in-depth data.

If you regularly enter your observations into the eBird database, you will be able to access your own bird records any time you want, allowing you to look at your observations in new ways and answer your own questions about what birds you saw, and when and where you saw them. You can use eBird as your primary long-term personal record or you can use it as a parallel record to the one you keep on your home computer.

Ultimately, the specific tools you use don't really matter; the important thing is that you keep records, and that you share them with the world birding community.

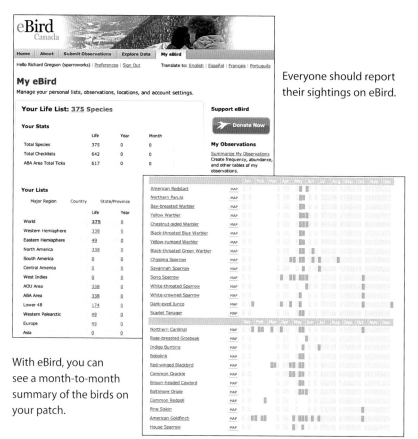

Everyone should report their sightings on eBird.

With eBird, you can see a month-to-month summary of the birds on your patch.

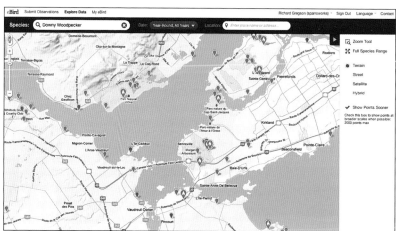

You can also search for recent sightings of specific birds in your area.

"As spring begins to break here at Braddock, I have managed to pick up a few migrant birds each morning and today I finally broke through the hundred barrier. The Bigby birding gods must have been with me this morning though as I broke through 100 birds in some style. Perhaps it was birding karma for popping out early to check and see if the pelicans had over-nighted at Salmon Creek (they had) in order to get a message on Genesee Birds to let people know they were still out there. As I pulled back into the drive this morning after checking the pelicans, I heard the distinctive grunt of Sandhill Cranes and lo and behold there were two of them drifting over my head and out towards the lake—a great Bigby score!"

—Luke Tiller (http://underclearskies.com)

The "Sport" of
Green Birding

5

N
ow we come to the "sport" of birding, and the activity from which the green birding idea first developed: listing. The ultimate contest is, as we will discuss shortly, the Big Year, in which a birder attempts to see as many species as possible in a single calendar year. The amount of effort that goes into that varies with the competitive instincts of the birder and his or her financial situation and need to work five days a week. However, if you can't put in the effort for a Big Green Bird Year there are several alternatives.

Most birders, whether they will admit to it or not, are somewhat competitive people who enjoy comparing their lists and sightings with other birders. In order to see "good" birds and add species to their lists, most list-keeping birders have usually been prepared to travel considerable distances to see them. Driving 100 or 200 miles to try to see a rare bird, the existence of which has been posted on a local birders' chat group, is not at all out of the ordinary in today's birding community. When participating in competitions such as Big Years, birders can travel thousands of miles (a considerable number of birders have traveled more than 100,000 miles on their Big Year birding ventures). But you can conduct a Big Year within your own town, county, or state and compete with others in each of these categories. A Big Green Big Year (Bigby) would be restricted to the places you can reach under your own steam.

You don't have to contribute greenhouse gases to the atmosphere to achieve a great list. In 2007, Wendy and Malkolm Boothroyd and their teenage son Ken Madsen attempted a really big Big Green Big Year (perhaps the ultimate Bigby to date although it is tricky to classify, as they had a strong support team with them who traveled by car) by cycling over 10,000 miles to see more than 500 species over the year. They started in their home province of the Yukon Territory and rode down the Pacific Coast, looping back around Arkansas to enjoy the Texas spring migration, then carried on eastward to

To be honest, if an Elegant Trogon appears on your patch, then you live in a very remote area on the Mexican border—or you have cycled there. A sighting of one of these rare, gorgeous birds would make all the effort worthwhile.

finish in Florida. By the end of their year, they had covered more than 13,000 miles by bicycle and tallied 548 species, raising more than 25,000 dollars for bird conservation in the process.

You can get a great list as a local green birder as well. When I did my first Bigby, in 2008, I walked and biked almost entirely within my 7-kilometer circle of my home and still ticked off 131 species. I'm not breaking any records here, I know, but it was still something to be proud of—and more importantly, a very enjoyable and satisfying year. More on that story later.

GREEN BIRDING LISTING CATEGORIES

People love to compete and compare their achievements; this is no less the case for birders than it is for athletes and art collectors. Comparing our lists with others only works well if there is some consistency to the way each list has been compiled. As you can imagine, as soon as birders first started to make green birding lists, they began to discuss rules. The American Birding Association has long had an agreed-on set of conditions governing the lists that they accept—but they don't have a separate category for green lists yet, so we in the green birding community have to handle this ourselves. After a good deal of discussion (where would we be without internet chat groups?) most people's ideas coalesced around some reasonable ways of adapting the traditional listing categories to green birding.

But first, a word on rules

Firstly, these are not rules. We couldn't enforce them even if we wanted to. Let's call them guidelines. There have been discussions, sometimes heated ones, about the acceptability of incorporating scheduled public transport into our green birding activities. Some say that any internal combustion engine adds to climate change and should therefore be eschewed, while others argue that the buses are going where they are going with or without you aboard, so you are doing no harm by taking them.

This is a contentious issue, but a consensus appears to have emerged that most green birders have found they could live with. This is that public transport is acceptable provided that the birder makes it plain that they have used it while compiling their lists.

The generally acceptable public transport options are local scheduled bus, ferry, and train services. Of course, there are differences of opinion: some birders believe all public transit is unacceptable, most are fine with local routes, and some will occasionally take longer rides by rail or Greyhound bus. Where you draw the line is up to you—just remember that "birding your patch" is really what this is all about.

Planes, taxis, and lifts from friends and relatives are universally considered to be unacceptable. By using a taxi or accepting a ride from a friend, you are creating a trip that otherwise wouldn't have been taken, and this is essentially the same as using your own car. No cheating please, however tired you are at the end of a long day! Planes are discounted by everyone because, even though they are scheduled services, their emission rates are so high no green birder wants to encourage them—most people tell me they just don't think it would feel right.

No naming convention for public transport-assisted lists has emerged yet (one wit proposed calling them "greenish" big years/days); for simplicity I would suggest that you add (PT) to any list that you contributed to using public transport. Thus, if you hopped a bus during your Big Green Big Year, then it is a Big Green Big Year (PT). Many birders keep two lists running side by side for their Bigby years. One is all the birds they saw in the year and the other is the ones that did not involve public transport. Just don't hide the way you made your list, that's all. There's nothing wrong with taking the bus, but for a level playing field we need to know how you collected your stupendous list—especially if we plan to beat you next year.

Now for the details of the categories. Of course, these are simply some popular challenges that green birders have come up with—you can do what you want if you think of a different or better way to play the game.

Big Green Big Year (BGBY, or Bigby)

This is the big one in the green birding word. In fact, this list's acronym (and its pronunciation, suggested by Canadian ornithologist Marcel Gahbauer) gave rise to the term "bigby" or "bigbying," a word that has come to be used as a sort of shorthand for any form of green birding.

In this challenge—the granddaddy of them all and one that requires a high degree of commitment—you will keep a count of all species of birds you see during a calendar year without using any gas. Thus you can walk, bike, canoe, ski, and so on in search of birds. You must start each birding trip at your regular residence or regular place of work (you can keep separate sublists for each); vacation birds should not be included. A true Bigby relates to the birds that you can see within reach of your home—though the fitter you are, the wider that circle of opportunity can be. There are birders, for example, who have set out on weekend and weeklong cycling trips covering hundreds of miles to add birds to their Bigbys, but as they started and ended at home, that's okay.

Remember that if you take a regularly scheduled bus or train during the year, then your Bigby is reclassified to become a "greenish" or a "semi-green" one.

At the moment the known Bigby record for an individual birder is held by Jim Royer of California and stands at 318 species seen in 2010.

The Yellow-billed Magpie has a rather restricted range in central and northern California; not many green birders will have them on their lists, but they are certainly worth a long cycle ride to find.

Walking Bigby

This is the same as above but you deliberately restrict your means of travel to walking only. This hardcore variant has evolved by popular demand; some birders want to make their lists really hard and so voluntarily restrict their birding to a single, specific mode of transport. The same requirement to start and finish at home holds. Of course, in any calendar year you could create a master Bigby list that includes all your green birds, with separate sub-lists for walking and cycling birds.

Green Big Day

This is a very popular challenge indeed; it is not too demanding (on your time or your body) and easily lends itself to friendly competition and sponsored fund-raising for charities.

The rules are similar to those of a yearlong Bigby in that you will be starting and finishing from home or your regular place of work. You will be birding for a 24-hour day and the usual rules about mode of transport apply. It is allowable to start or end your 24-hour GBD somewhere other than your home as long as you used no gas to get there and don't use any to return home afterwards (however tired you may be). Scheduled public transport helps a lot here and if you only use it for getting to and from your starting and ending points it won't downgrade your Green Big Day into a Semi-green one or a GBD(PT).

Conventionally, the 24-period has been midnight to midnight, but increasingly birders are opting for a 6 A.M. start and finish or a shortened day of dawn to dusk. It's up to you.

Birders in Montreal are experimenting with a team competition that adds a twist: a single well-known birding hot-spot is nominated and any competing birder or team of birders must visit it at least once during the 24-hour period. This ensures that final results are more comparable, and works especially well in big cities with their mix of habitats.

Some cyclists have had more than 160 species in a single Green Big Day. A few—mostly those very, very fit birders fortunate enough to live in California—have exceeded those numbers.

Semi-green Big Day

A variation of the Green Big Day, the Semi-green Big Day is birding for a 24-hour day and using no fuel during the count period, but starting and finishing anywhere; it doesn't matter how you got to the starting point.

In costal areas like Morrow Bay, California, birds can be spectacularly numerous and diverse.

This option allows you to do a Big Day while on vacation, for example. Let's be honest, only the most dedicated birder is actually going to stop taking vacations to reduce emissions, and when we are away from home we still want to see birds, don't we?

Depending on where you do your Semi-green Big Day, you can tick off astounding numbers of birds. The best record that I know of was gained by Ted Parker and Scott Robinson, who had 331 species in Tambopata National Reserve, Peru, in 1982. That is unlikely to be matched in most parts of North America and Europe, but between 100 and 150 species ought to be eminently achievable.

Green Big Sit

The Big Sit is a well-established and really enjoyable listing game during which you try to identify and count all the birds you see and hear in one day (or one hour) without moving from within a circle 17 feet in diameter. To make your Big Sit a truly green one you have to get to your count circle under your own power by walking, cycling, or so on.

You are only allowed to count birds that you see or hear from within the circle. If you see or hear a bird from within the circle but you can't truly identify it, then it is permissible to leave the circle and scout it out to confirm your identification. But if while you are out of the circle you happen across some other bird that you would dearly, dearly like to count, too bad! You have to return to the circle and just hope it comes closer.

An alternative is to restrict the time period to a set number of hours. Just doing a Big Sit for one (well-chosen) hour is very common and lends itself well to a club contest where you want to involve as many contestants as possible.

Don't ask why it's a 17-foot circle—it just is and always has been.

Big Foot Hour

This is an interesting new challenge. Try to see how many species you can find in one hour without using any gas. It is okay to start or finish somewhere away from home as long as you don't use gas on either leg.

Keith Hansen and Peter Pyle reported having seen 83 species in Bolinas, California, in one hour.

Variant green lists

You can make this competitive habit just as complex or as simple as you like. As we all know, the really inveterate lister will happily make a list out of anything—the more bizarre, the better, it often seems. The general green birding rules, of course, apply to the following examples—and you can add your own alternatives if there is not enough here to keep you occupied.

- Only birds seen—hearing them does not count
- Only birds heard, excluding those seen unless they were also heard
- Birds in your garden
- Birds seen from your office window
- Winter birds (a three-month list from December to February)
- Birds seen while walking your dog/accompanying your father to church/on the way to school
- List bird families as well as species

. . . and so on. You get the idea.

PLANNING YOUR GREEN BIG DAY

Attempting a Big Day is not only enjoyable, it is a splendid and intensive means of honing your field identification skills and really getting to know the patch of land on which you are birding. Not a minute is wasted.

If you were planning to do a traditional Big Day you would probably get together with two or three other birders and spend weeks poring over maps, working out the sites that you need to visit to maximize your chances of seeing the longest bird list possible for the time of year. On the great day you would be preparing to drive perhaps hundreds of miles, collecting speeding tickets along the way (I know from sad and expensive experience that the police do not consider the burning need to get a Barred Owl and a Spotted Sandpiper before breakfast to be an adequate reason for breaking the law); while you would certainly have a wonderful time you would be behaving in about as un-green a way as it is possible to do.

For a Green Big Day, you are going to plan things a little differently.

Whether you start and end the counting at midnight (the conventional way) or decide to bird dawn to dawn or dusk to dusk, a Big Day is a *long* day, especially if the birds are playing hard-to-get. I suggest that you find at least one other person to do the day with you and help to keep your spirits up. It's good if they are a birder too, but it could simply be someone who enjoys your company and will help out by keeping the tally or carrying your spotting scope. Having a friend along will ensure that you finish the course and don't get discouraged.

First of all, decide whether your GBD is going to be restricted to your local routes and patch, or if you will widen your circuit somewhat by using public transport (a Semi-green Big Day). Maybe you'll consider doing two GBDs—one with and one without the help of scheduled bus services. If you choose to make use of public transport you can start somewhere far from home if you wish—but don't forget that you must use the public transport to get home again after your day has finished, and there may not be many services running at midnight.

You also need to think about the best time of year to do your GBD. Where I am birding in southern Quebec, that almost certainly means the second half of May, when the spring migration is in full flow and new species are arriving daily before continuing through to the boreal forests north of us. In other parts of the world, other factors may come into play. You are the expert in your local bird movements and can best judge the time of year when you have the chance of seeing the most birds. Birding is never a waste of time whenever you do it, but selecting the peak time of the year for your area is really essential for getting a good list—it would really be rather dispiriting to attempt your GBD in midsummer when half the birds are keeping quiet and avoiding the heat.

Next, scout your intended area thoroughly before the chosen day. You only have a day to get these birds in and you can't afford to waste a moment, but nothing beats good planning and good local knowledge. Figure out what species you could see and divide them into two groups—the easy ones that you know you can find without too much difficulty and the rarer species that you will need to get to make up the optimal GBD list. Chickadees? Not a problem. But where will you find a Great Horned Owl or a Scarlet Tanager or a Grasshopper Sparrow? Those are the birds whose territories you want to try to locate in advance.

Keep in mind that part of your GBD (several hours if you're going for the full 24 hours) is going to be in the dark. What birds can you realistically expect to record in the small hours? There are actually a lot, but you will want to spend some time in preparation, making sure that you can identify them by their calls and songs; the chances of actually *seeing* any birds in the dark are low to non-existent. Perhaps you have a riverside or an area of marshland in your vicinity? That would be a good place to start your chase. It is amazing just how noisy a marsh can be in the dark, and and you can collect a dozen or more easy birds, if you're lucky, to get you off to a decent start. Rails and bitterns, nighthawks and Whip-poor-wills can be found if you pick the right spot. Then there are the nocturnal owl species that can be heard on a clear night and which will often reveal themselves by responding to a call; practice your owl imitations or take along a (judiciously and sparingly used) recording and a small speaker. Owls are not always the rarities people think; they are just discreet.

Around dawn you will start to pick up a sudden burst of species as the light wakes them up and the dawn chorus begins. You know your area—the best place for early-light birding might be a lake, marshy area, mixed forest, or open grassland. Make sure that you and your friend(s) have the place spotted and well scouted and that you are there at dawn waiting for the birds to show themselves. A thermos of coffee helps the count mount at this point.

Marsh Wrens can be seen in winter in the southern states and in summer in the northern states and Canada. This one was a two-hour bike ride from my home, but it made the whole trip worth the effort.

After the early-morning rush things will slow down until later in the day. Your planned and scouted route therefore needs to be directed toward finding target birds at this stage—that is, single species that you have not picked up in the early rush and that you have a good idea of where to find. And, of course, they need to be ones you can access by foot of cycle (or bus, if you're doing a Semi-green Big Day). This is the point when that friendly companion comes into play and keeps you encouraged and focused.

Gradually the day will pick up, and as late afternoon slides into dusk the pace will pick up again as you tick off those birds you missed earlier in the day. You will have planned your route so that you are in the right place at the right time but there will still be birds that you expected to get but have so far not succeeded in doing so. Think carefully—do you go after the two rarities to prove that you could find them or do you try for the six common birds you ought to have ticked but have not yet found? Only you can make that strategic decision. One is good for the soul; one is good for the list. Both might be possible if you have scouted your area thoroughly enough.

Finally, the day winds down and you decide you have got all the birds you are going to get. Walk or cycle home (or take the bus if you're doing a semi-green day), have that meal and drink you promised yourself, and add up your species list. Report it to your green birding website/forum and tell your friends, write it up for your club newsletter or blog, and do what you can to publicize your efforts.

Then start planning for next year, because you can always do better. Green Big Days are hard work but they do only last a day, and they are strangely compulsive once you have been bitten by the bug.

Making the Big Day competitive

There's nothing like a bit of competition to turn a fun birding day into an especially memorable one—nor, indeed, for cementing friendships among birders.

In western Canada, in the Okanagan Valley, an annual birding Big Day contest first organized in 1986 is now one of the premier events of the kind in North America. This Big Day (and its accompanying "Little Big Day") is held on the Sunday of the Canadian Victoria Day weekend (the Sunday just before May 24) and is also a major fund-raiser for birding projects and conservation charities. It is also, these days, an entirely green Big Day event—well, there is a minor exception, but the rules still prevent the 1,000-mile marathons that some contests seem to involve.

I include here the basic rules that Dick Cannings established for the Okanagen event as they provide a very good template for the sort of the Green Big Day contest that you and your birding friends might consider organizing. With suitable amendments for local conditions and preferences

Okanagan Big Day Challenge Rules

- Teams must have a name. If you don't have a team name before you start, you must think one up during the day. Usually after 20+ hours of straight birding, something appropriate will surface.
- Teams can consist of any number of birders, though 2 to 6 is ideal. Team members must remain within earshot of each other throughout the day.
- This is a green event, so birders must travel on bicycle or by foot. If a car has to be used, the team must remain within a 24-kilometer diameter circle (e.g. a Christmas Bird Count circle). There are different categories for each type of transportation.
- Teams must begin and end the day within [insert the boundaries of your local area/town/county]
- No tape recorders are allowed to attract birds (they are recommended, however, for documenting a calling or singing rarity), although the participants may imitate bird calls by whistles, grunts, hoots, or whatever.
- A participant may join or leave a team partway through the day, as long as he or she is part of the team for at least half of the time that team spends in the field. For example, a person who is not too keen on getting up at 2:00 A.M. may join his or her team at dawn without that team having to delete species not seen by that person. A corollary of this is that the ABA's 95 percent rule does not apply. A person in the field for less than half of the time must act as a "nonparticipating companion" as defined and regulated in the ABA rules.
- All species seen or heard during the day must be checked off a checklist and the checklist submitted to the organizers before or during the brunch on Monday. Any species indicated as casual, accidental, or nonexistent at the current time of year on the local area checklist must be documented with a full field description, photograph, or tape recording, and this evidence must be submitted to and accepted by the organizers.

this would make a splendid local competition for just about anywhere, and I would commend these rules to guide anyone trying this venture.

Teams participating in the Big Day go out from midnight to midnight, while the Little Big Day competition involves teams going out for any 8-hour period on Sunday. The organizers arrange a potluck brunch the next morning, where all the participants trade stories of the previous day's adventures.

PLANNING A BIG GREEN BIG YEAR

Now let's go for the truly tough one. This is really going to test your mettle, but you are also going to have a lot of fun and good birding as you proceed through the year. If you have ever done a traditional Big Year then you will find that for a Bigby you have to be a bit more creative to get some of the more unusual or rare species . . . but that simply makes the process that much more interesting and challenging.

How you go about planning your year will vary depending on your fitness and experience and the geography of the place in which you live. It would be a waste of time for me to give you hard and fast rules as to how to go about this, as you know your territory, and I don't. Nevertheless, a few ideas about how to plan ought to set you on the right track to success.

The first step is to decide how you're going to travel. Do you want to make your Bigby an entirely walking or cycling one, or will you allow yourself the occasional bus ride? This will affect all your planning, so decide on this now.

Start making your plans by getting yourself a really good map of the area you will be birding in. You'll want a good topographic map, one that shows

Use Google Maps for a bird's-eye view of your area to help identify attractive habitat for birds.

If your birding territory is on one of the flyways used each spring and fall by Snow Geese, you will not have much trouble adding them to your list. They travel a long way, and many green birders will be able to look out for them.

tracks and trails and land contours as well as roads. Back it up by making good use of the features offered by Google Maps and Google Earth; their satellite and street views are exceptionally useful in planning should there be a corner in your territory that you are not familiar with.

You can safely assume that anywhere that you can reach under your own power on a weekend or while walking the dog before work is somewhere that you can probably cover quite easily in all seasons—so now think further afield. Identify the good birding sites in your larger area and then find out which ones you can reach on foot or bicycle and which you will need to make use of public transport to get to. Check the transport timetables—can you take a bus there in time for the early and bird-rich morning, or will you have to come up the night before and stay overnight in order to bird effectively? Is there a campground or a bed and breakfast nearby?

Next, think about the habitat in these more distant sites and the birds that they (should) hold. Figure out which season or seasons you need to visit these areas in and fix them in your diary. These birding hotspots will form the backbone of your Big Year. For example, you might want to visit an area of mixed woodland in the spring warbler migration season and a lake or marsh when the ducks or Snow Geese are arriving. Decide where you are going to be and when and commit to actually being there. Book your accommodations, if necessary, plan your route, check the bus schedule, and pray for favorable weather.

After that, turn your thoughts to your main patch. You know this area better than anyone, so write down the birds that you expect to see and the times of year most likely to find them. Are there birds that breed on your patch? Those you probably have plenty of time to tick off—but what about the migratory birds that just drop by for a few days in spring and fall? Concentrate on being available to see these birds when they are most likely to be there, because your chasing abilities are limited. Work your patch to death, morning, noon, and night in all seasons, remembering that if a certain species only passes through once in the year you only have one chance to add it to your Bigby list.

The more ordinary birding opportunities can be fitted around these larger efforts. When I did a Bigby for the first time I was raring to go on January first, but the weather was pretty bad and I restricted myself to a very cold two-hour walk around my neighborhood, slipping and sliding on the snow and ice as I went. Still, I came home with my first handful of species safely ticked off—birds that I no longer had to worry about for the other 364 days of the year. They weren't all common birds, either. There were a couple of species around that day that I thought I might have trouble collecting; had I not been out walking this rather unexciting route on that particular day, I might have missed them altogether. Remember that you can't see birds if you are not out birding, so plan to get out frequently between the longer expeditions. Walking to work, the local store, or the bus stop; exercising the dog or the children—all these are opportunities on which you just might pick up a bird you never expected.

But life is not all birding—certainly the rest of your family will be thinking that way not too many weeks into your Big Year. Don't neglect your garden and your yardwork—but stay conscious of birds while pulling weeds or picking fruit. Was that a hawk that flew over? What's that over there by the pond or at the top of the lilac bush? A well-planned and decently stocked garden is a Bigbyist's best friend because it will pull in a remarkable number of birds during the year which you can then tick off from your lawnchair in the shade. See chapter 6 for more about managing your garden for birds.

Above all, don't give up. Walk, cycle, paddle, and take the bus. Twelve months of interest and excitement lie ahead of you—and none of it will be adding to the carbon content of our atmosphere!

A TYPICAL BIG GREEN BIG YEAR

What would a local Big Green Big Year entail and what might you expect to see and experience? What is the experience like and what does it involve? Is it *really* fun, or is this something that you do because you think you ought to?

f you search the internet you will find quite a number of blogs and single blog posts by birders who have attempted Bigbys or similar challenges. Here are just a few good places to start:

http://ocbirding.blogspot.com/2010/01/bigby-to-end-all-bigbys.html
http://bikebybirding.blogspot.com/
http://greenbirding.blogspot.com/
http://christiannunesbgby.blogspot.com/

The best thing I can do to give you an idea of how a Big Green Big Year might pan out is to tell you about my own first Bigby. This Bigby was done in 2008, about the time that the whole green birding phenomenon was starting to bubble to the collective surface and people all over the world were adding their names to the online registry.

I am not going to tell you about a grand effort to capture the world record undertaken by a super-athlete capable of cycling 100 miles a day. Rather I am going to tell you about my own attempt to see what I could see in a year around a fairly typical suburban area on the edges of a major city—in this case, Montreal. I am not a competitive person; I do my birding out of a love of birds and interest in the world around me and because I believe this is important. This was a Bigby that I believe is practical and achievable by any averagely experienced birder who has—and haven't we all—other things in life in addition to birding. (Think how long our lists could be if we did not have to work five days a week!)

If I could do it, then you could undoubtedly do better.

So let's set the scene. It is New Year's Day, January 1, in the year 2008. I am fortunate in that I live in a fairly leafy suburb on the western end of Montreal island, with easy access to the St. Lawrence River and a large arboretum. I have two good legs, a bicycle, a canoe, and a keen birding wife (these things are always easier and more pleasant if shared). And I had told my birding friends, "I am doing a Bigby this year," so I was committed with no chance of backing out. I had decided to see how many birds I could see by restricting myself primarily to walking, with just the occasional foray forth on a cycle and a couple of canoe trips at key times of the year. I would mostly be walking, though, and definitely not taking public transport (though that has become an accepted green birding option).

The year started with a big, cold, white dump of snow that severely limited any attempts to get out and about. On New Year's Day, I managed to count a grand total of just 8 species by walking the neighborhood streets well bundled up (it was minus 25 degrees Celsius, or 13 below in Fahrenheit). People doing Bigbys in California had already reported bird counts up to and even surpassing 100 species for the day. By January 3, though, the days had turned very bright, very sunny, and intensely cold, which brought a few new birds to my garden feeders. Garden feeders are crucial to the success of a Bigby such as this—feeders in a bird-friendly garden with plenty of the things growing there that birds like. Clearly it was going to be a slow start to the birding year—and a frustrating one, too, because I already knew that there was a gorgeous adult male Snowy Owl just a half hour's drive away and I was sorely, sorely tempted. Before my conversion to green birding, I would have been after it in a heartbeat, but I resisted. It wasn't as if it were a lifer, after all.

A couple of days later I made it about 3 miles by bicycle to the wonderful Morgan Arboretum to walk the snowshoe trail for the first time that winter. It was a beautiful day—not too cold, lovely snow . . . and not too many birds, to be honest. A long view of a Pileated Woodpecker hacking at a tall tree was perhaps the bird of the day (and a new bird for the year list).

January 12 and—"O frabjous day! Callooh! Callay!" as the man in Lewis Caroll's "Jabberwocky" sang—a Carolina Wren visited our garden in the early afternoon to scrabble about in the leaf litter under the deck looking for food. Managing to always keep some small branch or twig between him and the autofocus on my camera, he remained undocumented on this initial visit but later, around 4 P.M., he returned briefly and I managed to catch a couple of rapid confirmatory images. Those who live in more southern, sunnier climes will doubtless be wondering what all the fuss was about, but up here on the northern limits of its range this species is truly a rarity which we have only seen at all in the past few years. In fact, it is only because of climate change that we are seeing any at all—good for the birder's life list, not so good for the planet, perhaps.

That Carolina Wren was a great boost to my efforts, though. A few days later, my wife and I were walking along the riverside and added a pair of Pine Grosbeaks perched high in a tree in the neighboring town of Sainte-Anne-de-Bellevue. This was especially good as they are an irruptive species not often seen around here; we usually hear them once or twice up in the arboretum but never quite this close to home, and some years we totally *dip out* on the species (that's birder jargon for *fail to see*). A very good tick, Bigby or not. My wife had bought me a pedometer at Christmas in the hope that it would encourage me to do the famous 10,000 steps per day and keep fit—and for the record, those two birds cost 7,395 steps.

After two weeks of a cold and snowy Bigby, my personal count stood at a paltry 18 species: Rock Dove, Mourning Dove, Downy Woodpecker, Hairy Woodpecker, Carolina Wren, American Robin, Black-capped Chickadee,

Red-breasted Nuthatch, White-breasted Nuthatch, Blue Jay, American Crow, European Starling, Dark-eyed Junco, Northern Cardinal, Pine Grosbeak, House Finch, American Goldfinch, and House Sparrow. Still fifty weeks to go in the year—*nil desperandum*. I consoled myself with the knowledge that a large number of those many, many birds being seen in California and other places in the south would have to come to Canada to breed later in the year. It's all a matter of being in the right place at the right time.

And so January continued with the odd new bird here and there, but I was only into the mid-20s as the month ended, with Common Redpolls having been the bogey bird thus far. Neighbors and friends had been reporting flocks everywhere—up the road, down the road . . . they were simply never there when we were there. However fast we got on the trail after a report, their busy little flocks had moved along, as they do. Then suddenly, early one morning as I was brewing the dawn coffee, the garden was full of them! Not only that, but a small number of the much, much less common Hoary Redpolls had come along. A wonderful start to the day and end to the month!

February. Due to the really cold winter we had (Montreal had the deepest snowfall on record that year) and our determination not to get into the car to chase some really excellent reports of "good" birds, birding was really hard work and every additional species had to be fought for. For two or three depressing weeks, my list remained firmly stuck at 25 species. There was a Pileated Woodpecker in the neighborhood (you will recall I had seen one in the arboretum) that my wife kept seeing but which evaded me constantly— soon, I told myself. The registered Bigbyists down in the southern U.S. were reporting high numbers, with those along the California coast areas starting to pass 200 species already—something that would be impossible hereabouts, even for the full year. What was particularly interesting from reading the postings by people doing Bigbies was how many people were seeing unsuspected birds close to their own homes which they never knew were there simply because they used to go out birding by car to a destination birding site.

By the third week of the month the sun was starting to shine at a slightly more elevated angle, and out of the wind you could actually feel some heat in its rays. Combine that with the male cardinals I'd heard calling from their territories on a couple of mornings and the Great Horned Owl in the Arboretum who was telling others to keep their distance from his nesting site, and I started to suspect that the year was moving along as it should. It was still cold, but it no longer felt as "wintery" as it did, and the birds were slowly starting to respond to the changes.

At the end of February, despite many desperate attempts to spot the Pileated Woodpeckers that were within a few hundred yards of my house, they were still resolutely refusing to show themselves to me (although I *had* finally heard them calling and so could tick them off for the year). On

I am a keen fly fisherman as well as a birder. One day I just happened to put down my rod and pick up my camera at just the right moment to catch this Common Loon surfacing with a trout.

February 23, we took a Bigby stroll along the river to Sainte-Anne-de-Belle-vue where, out on the old canal locks, I added a Great Black-backed Gull (there was open water by the rapids there), soon followed by two Common Loons. Excellent—and what was more, the presence of the loons indicated that the odd bird was starting to move back north, despite the ever-present snow. Shortly after lunch, a Sharp-shinned Hawk arrived in the garden, looked around and spotted a pair of goldfinches clinging, terrified, to one of our feeders. It swooped low over the birds, causing them to panic and fly up into the air, then swung around and simply snatched one of them on the wing. It took it up into a maple tree and ripped it apart. It was a spectacular addition to the year list.

In March, the bird sightings slowly continued to accumulate, with two more Carolina Wrens, a flock of Cedar Waxwings, Red-winged Blackbirds, and an early Song Sparrow. On March 23, I saw my first House Sparrow of the winter—something that says much about their decline, as only a few years ago they were regulars. Later in the day, another visit to the locks at Sainte-Anne-de-Bellevue yielded a small flock of Common Goldeneye and another pair of Common Loons. Any water birds in search of open water at this time of year have pretty well got to come here if they are in the vicinity so it's always worth checking out. Sure enough, when I visited again a week later, I got four new species for the year list: Canvasbacks, Canada Geese, and a Common Grackle at the locks, and then, as we were almost back home, a lot of crow noise helped us to add a gorgeous Red-tailed Hawk.

With the first quarter of a year gone, I started April with hopes that things would soon start to look up. I spent a pleasant five minutes one day in the company of a Hermit Thrush in the arboretum, having had one of the same species earlier in the day in my own garden. Near the end of the month, the goldfinches really began to glow as their rather drab olive-green winter plumage was replaced by the typical flaming yellow breeding plumage.

In early May I started to get twitchy, waiting for the rush of spring migrants that normally peaks hereabouts in the second half of the month. A pleasant weekend day saw a cycle expedition around the margins of Montreal island to see what might be found in a wider area than I could visit on foot; I managed to tick off more than thirty species . . . numbers were suddenly starting to increase dramatically. In the bay at Anse-à-l'Orme we were treated to the sight of a solitary Osprey flying overhead.

Things really got hot the next week. As part of my Bigby, I had agreed to lead a walking Big Day as part of a sponsored fund-raiser for a local migratory bird-banding station, the McGill Bird Observatory. This is an operation dear to my heart that does the valuable research work of netting and banding birds as they pass through the area. There were about 15 people in the group on that gloriously warm and sunny day. We started at the observatory, walked many of the forest trails in the adjacent arboretum, and then spread out along the lakeshore. By the end of this intensive day I had raised my Bigby list to 50 species while walking and 68 species while cycling—allowing for some overlap between the two groups, I had a personal total of 92 species.

Around mid-June things began to slow down as far as my ability to add new species to the year list went. I was working in a fairly restricted area, even with the occasional extended cycle trip, and most birds were hunkered down in their nests making new birds. So I took a vacation, did some gardening, things like that.

Around the middle of July it started to become evident that the gardens, the arboretum, and the open spaces were rapidly filling up with legions of scruffy young birds eagerly harassing their parents for food, food, and more food—NOW! Finally, the elusive local Pileated Woodpecker took pity on me and paid an extended visit to one of our garden peanut feeders to stock up on high-calorie food, which it then proceeded to stuff down the throat of its demanding youngster who was tagging along. A couple of days before this we had a similar display of parental nut-stuffing by a male Northern Cardinal and his kid. You'd think that when teenage birds get to adult size they'd go off and fend for themselves, but it doesn't work like that. For cardinals, at least, once the dad finally does get this lump of teenage "gimme" off his hands, he'll probably go off and produce another brood before the fall.

Summer is a quiet time for bird listing, but the above is a good example of the fun you can have as a birder when you are not busy ticking new species off your year list. A lot of the pleasure and interest of birding comes from simply watching them going about their business, studying their behavior and learning about what makes them tick.

July turned into August. I did plenty of walking and cycling after birds, but not many new species to add to the list until around mid-August, when the water levels on the river began to fall, revealing wide expanses of mud. These are highly attractive to the small shorebirds that were already starting to migrate south again. One evening my wife and I visited the shores of Anse-à-l'Orme Nature Park, on the northwestern shore of Montreal island (a good long cycle ride away), and saw a very fine selection of little guys skittering about: Solitary Sandpiper, Greater Yellowlegs, Least Sandpiper, Killdeer, and Semipalmated Sandpiper. Anse-à-l'Orme is a shallow bay, and it takes only a small drop in water levels to expose great expanses of the muddy, sandy habitat beloved of shorebirds. In addition to the birds noted above, we enjoyed several flocks of Red-winged Blackbirds starting to gather (signaling that the end of summer was near), a couple of Great Blue Herons, a Belted Kingfisher, and various other birds including a fine Eastern Kingbird.

And then—one of the pleasures of serendipitous green birding—we had an incredible sighting. A russet bird with white and black streaked out of a reed bed right in front of us and dived out of sight into more vegetation. "Wazzat?!" we cried and, confirming we had both seen the same field marks, grabbed our copy of the field guide. Given the territory and behavior, it could only have been a Red-necked or else a Horned Grebe—both pretty uncommon hereabouts, though occasionally seen in migration at the end of the season. "Ah well," we thought, "it's one or the other," when damn me if it didn't fly back again and pretty well clinch itself as being a Horned Grebe. We never did see it on the water because of the high reeds but it could not have been anything else. It breeds out west and in the Iles de la Madeleine north of my patch, but certainly not hereabouts, so we counted this as a good tick indeed. The migration seasons are certainly the times for serious rarities.

At the end of August a friend told me that he had seen a "tree full of Blackpoll Warblers" in the morning. I congratulated him and hoped they would come my way. Over my ritual end-of-day, after-work cup of tea, a Cedar Waxwing dropped by the garden and then three Magnolia Warblers, a Red-eyed Vireo, and a Warbling Vireo. The autumn migration had indeed begun.

The next week saw the start of September and a small inrush of early-morning birds, including Blackpoll Warbler, Canada Warbler, Black-throated Green Warbler, a large flock of Cedar Waxwings, and American Robins—plus a bunch of European Starlings and a couple Blue Jays, some chickadees, a few Song Sparrows . . . and so on. All from simply strolling around—no cars were needed to find these excellent birds.

As days passed, a couple of moderate-sized flights of Canada Geese went south during the day reminding me that winter would come soon. Searching my patch turned up Red-eyed Vireo and a Nashville Warbler. Out on the shoreline more shorebirds were still turning up and the occasional duck started to drop by. One evening I saw a small flotilla of Wood Ducks paddling around some reeds along the riverbank at the end of my road while the golden sun illuminated them as it touched the horizon.

By the end of September we had passed the autumnal equinox and, despite the bright sunshine, the wind moved more to the north and nights became a little colder, with a touch of frost a couple of days. The birdlife was notably less populous and flights of southbound geese were regularly appearing in the skies.

On October 4 my wife and I did the "Sparroworks Birding Trail" in the arboretum. The weather was quite chilly and the skies were gray, but ornithologically it was a glorious day, with the first showings of fall and winter bird species moving down from the north. We saw several Hermit Thrushes, mostly mixed in with flocks of robins, one Wood Thrush, early Dark-eyed Juncos, a small group of White-crowned Sparrows, Ruby-crowned Kinglets, various warblers, and so forth. The stars of the day were a number of Winter Wrens (we actually had 7 in sight together at one point) working the crevices of a log pile in front of the sugar shack. Some people find this pile of old wood unsightly and have been making efforts to have it moved—yet every year it is full of insectivorous birds and assorted mice and chipmunks.

In mid-October, I took in one of Bird Protection Quebec's weekly guided field trips in the arboretum. It was a beautiful sunny day with blue skies and plenty of color in the trees still. Jolly chilly in the early morning, though, and I decided it would probably be my last birding trip sans gloves until the next spring. We were especially pleased to see the first of the Pine Siskins, as they were absent last winter, being an irruptive species that is not always in this area every winter.

In November, a walk along the lakeshore at dusk added a Redhead and five male plus two female Bufflehead to the Bigby list for the year—numbers 121 and 122, respectively. I had been stuck at a round 120 species for a long time, and these two were well worth getting cold for.

The birding was very slow after that and it was quite hard work adding any new species to my list. In the first week of December I was scouting around some flat fields just west of Anse-á-l'Orme when a big shadow blocked out the sky and a Rough-legged Hawk flew overhead. Later I saw it, or rather, I think, a second one, flying low over the fields and then perching

Snow Buntings are a treat reserved for green birders who, like me, spend much of the winter in deep snow. These beautiful birds' large, twittering, fast-moving flocks come and go like the snow flurries.

in a distant tree. A flock of about 100 Horned Larks were in a field nearby, making the outing a very worthwhile one. As the year drew to a close, I saw two flocks of Snow Buntings and four American Tree Sparrows hiding from the weather in a line of trees. I continued to collect reasonable numbers of the last remaining hoped-for winter birds.

Finally, we came to the last day of 2008, which was graced by the appearance of that elusive, but always looked-for little bird, the Pine Siskin. I was glad to welcome them back.

And last, but not least, we were visited on the same day by a beautiful Pine Grosbeak—not a Bigby bird, as I had seen them around a couple of times back in January and February, but an addition to my personal garden list and very welcome bird any time.

My total for the year: 131 species, a lot of good memories, and a greatly enhanced appreciation of the excellent birding that can be done within a very short distance of my home.

Creating a
Green Bird Garden

6

I t may surprise you to find a chapter about gardening in a birding book—
but if you are going to be focusing on birds that you can reach without
using your car, then where better to start looking for them than at home?

In these days of rapid habitat loss, perhaps one of the best things that
green birders can do, both for the environment and for the richness of their
life lists, is to fashion their gardens in such a way that birds are attracted to
them. This is also an excellent means of ensuring that even on those days

when you have to stay close to home you will have some interesting birds to watch. Plus, there are no internal combustion engines involved, and absolutely no traveling. This is green birding at its simplest—and when you have made your wildlife garden you can later consider using it as the site for your Green Big Sit.

I don't know which pastime spoke to me first—birding or gardening. To be able to combine the two activities into one seems to me to be ideal. It doesn't have to be hard work—well, not especially so. Birds don't really like things too tidy, so you can leave some fallen leaves in a pile, not cut the grass as often as your neighbors do, pile some logs in a corner instead of chopping and hauling them, and generally take a rather more relaxed approach to the whole business than some people perhaps think you should. None of which means you have to accept a scruffy and an unkempt garden. Not at all—a bird or wildlife garden ought to be a garden for the soul as well as for the birds. Many times I have received visitors who I just knew were looking askance at our small plot and wondering where the regimented rows of annuals were, only to have them compliment us as they left on the pleasure they had taken in our "peaceful and attractive" garden. They also usually say nice things about the birds that have been sharing it with them.

Naturally, if you are blessed with a large rural property that is replete with trees and meadows then you hardly have to do anything at all; the birds are already there. Most of us don't have that luxury—but what you might not realize is that a suburban garden on a regular subdivision can be amazingly attractive to birds when yours is the only patch for miles around to have the things they are looking for. Even an apartment balcony can attract birds if you set about the business effectively. The effects of industrial agriculture on wildlife and wildlife habitat are often so pronounced that it has been said (perhaps cynically, yet with an element of truth) that the best way to improve biodiversity in a meadow is to build houses on it. In fact, many studies have shown that often the birdlife is healthier, happier, and present in larger numbers in suburban gardens than it is in the agricultural "countryside" surrounding many of our cities, simply because there is a greater diversity of plants, shelter, and available food in gardens than there is in the monocultural deserts that lie outside our communities.

Can your garden really attract interesting birds? As an example, my fairly average suburban garden of some 15,000 square feet has, after some careful planting and design changes, a species list in the region of 120. It may not be anything to boast about or even anything approaching a record, but it makes for some interesting and pleasant birding right outside my door.

When you start work on your bird garden, friends and neighbors are very likely to think you have given up and are letting your land go wild and

Small, fast-moving, and really hard to photograph, busy little Ruby-crowned Kinglets can be found all over. This fellow posed for his picture in my garden.

become overcome with weeds. They are mistaken, as they will realize when your plantings mature and they see the new birds arriving at your feeders. A wildlife garden is a special sort of place in the same way that some people have rose gardens, fruit gardens, or herb gardens. As it develops, and the birds and other wildlife come to find it, you will realize that you have actually created a small, private nature reserve.

A bird's wants are remarkably simple—food, shelter, and somewhere to raise young. All of those are relatively easy to provide once you decide to do something about it.

GETTING YOUR HANDS DIRTY

If you are creating a new garden, take time to really look at and think about the plot of land you are going to be working with. Pause to look at what grows locally in the wild and in other gardens in your area for ideas. Remember that you cannot force plants to grow where they don't want to, so look to see what already flourishes and where it likes to grow in your garden plot. If you find something growing naturally and wish to keep it, then leave it where it is instead of trying to move it.

Remember that birds, just like people, are seeking opportunities for food, shelter, and sex—but what the gardener sees is not necessarily what the birds see. To become a successful bird gardener you must learn to think and see like a bird. All too often, a tidy, "beautiful" garden for people is little better than a desert for the birds. Birds need a little clutter, a little comfortable disorder—but with some flexibility and a willingness to adjust your standards, your bird garden can still be a beautiful garden for people as well.

A successful bird garden needs to provide the following features:

- Food and water
- Shelter from both bad weather and predators
- Nesting opportunities
- Plantings at three levels—a mixed environment
- Something for ourselves, a place where we can sit and watch and perhaps photograph the birds

Let's look at a few of these features in more detail.

Feeding the birds

This book is not primarily about bird feeding, but it is important to getting plenty of birds to come to your garden. Having food available is essential to a good species count and is an easy factor to consider. Remember, though, that providing food is not simply a case of putting out bird feeders on poles—your garden plantings and the insects that live on your plants will always provide the bulk of the day-to-day food that your birds rely on.

You want to have a selection of feeder types: tray or ground feeders, hopper feeders, and tube feeders for large and small seeds.

Ground feeding can be as simple as scattering some seed on the ground. Or you can set up something tidier such as a mesh-floored tray on a frame supported on low legs. Sadly, you are also going to be feeding the squirrels with any attempt at ground feeding—but they can be fun, too. Just learn to accept them as the price of having ground-feeding birds.

Different birds have different ways they like to have their food presented to them. Tube feeders with the spiral perches are particularly effective for smaller bird species, while a hopper-style feeder with a tray at the bottom is terrific for mid-sized birds like cardinals. Chickadees will, of course, eat from anything!

Now that you've chosen a variety of feeders, you need to put some thought into where you will place them. Needless to say, you will want to put your feeders where you can see them. It's best to place them near some sort of shelter or security for birds such as shrubs, but not so near that squirrels or cats can leap onto the feeders. Finally, make sure they'll be accessible in winter—don't make keeping them stocked in deep snow a chore. Remember to keep the feeders and water bowls clean, as they cause birds to congregate and thereby increase the risk of them passing diseases to each other.

An assortment of feeders offering a variety of foods. The more types of feeders and foods you offer, especially in winter, the more species you will see in your garden.

It is obvious to experienced birders, but worth repeating, that different birds like different seeds. Present the wrong seed types and you will have few or no birds. Offer seeds of different sizes—niger for the goldfinches and siskins, sunflower for chickadees and Blue Jays, peanuts for woodpeckers and so on. Woodpeckers adore fat, waxwings go for fruit (on your trees), and orioles fancy fruit on the trees or on your feeder.

Should you feed birds all year round or only during the cold months? This common question is endlessly discussed. You should certainly offer food in winter, but there is no harm in feeding in summer as well. Birds will not come to depend on your offerings but will use the food to supplement the wild food growing elsewhere in your garden and around your wider birding patch.

Keep in mind that the main food sources in your nascent bird garden will be natural ones. You will want to make sure that your plantings provide plenty of seeds, berries, nectar, fruit, nuts, and buds (later in this chapter we'll discuss specific plants that are good for green bird gardens). Remember that your plants don't just have to attract birds directly, they can also attract the creatures that some birds like to eat: insects, worms, larvae, eggs, and rodents. Even some of the birds your garden attracts are going to serve as a food source attracting still other birds. Nothing is so cheering to the green birder on a cold winter's morning than to enjoy the sight of a Cooper's Hawk taking a plump Mourning Dove from your feeders and eating it on the snow in front of your dining room window while you sip your coffee. Who said that green birding always has to involve punishing exercise?

Water

Water, especially moving water, is a *huge* bird magnet. Nothing else that you place in your garden will have such an effect on the number of species you

Lots of birds will come to a garden pond.

A small waterfall can double the number of birds you see in your garden.

see as a puddle of water. Each spring during migration a dozen or more species of warblers and other migrating songbirds drop into my garden solely to visit our pond and small waterfall. It never fails.

But, you are saying, I don't have the space for a garden pond. Well, in a small garden or on an apartment balcony a container of water such as an inverted dustbin lid or even a bucket will draw birds—especially if they can access the water by perching on the rim or on stones or twigs placed inside it. There should be some low shrubs or other perching opportunities near to the water, because birds usually like to approach these features with some caution.

You could just very simply forego an actual pond for now and install a dripping tap or a slow trickle from the end of a hose. Your "catch" rate will increase tenfold—these things are like catnip to birds. In winter, also consider placing a heated birdbath somewhere where you can see it from your house. These are very effective.

Of course, a pond is better than a bucket or birdbath, but it doesn't by any means have to be huge. Small ponds will suffer more than large ones from problems with algae, but that is a solvable problem and the birds usually won't care. You can combat algae by *not* changing the water every spring, counterintuitive as that may seem. You want the nutrient level in the water to be low; fresh tap water is rich in the stuff that keeps algae blooming. You should also place some water lilies and other pond plants in there (talk to your garden center) that will shade the water and lower the light levels that algae require. If algae does appear after all that, there are safe algicides you can add to the water. Remarkably, a net of oat or barley straw (available from pond plant nurseries) submerged in the pond will also keep algae at bay by depleting the water of nutrients.

Waterfalls are the big must-have feature of the really productive bird garden. If you can manage to have some sort of moving water feature connected to your pond then the range of species that you see will be magnified many times. Moving water also helps to keep algae down and certainly reduces problems with mosquitoes—which will not lay their eggs in moving water.

Still water, however, provides egg-laying opportunities to mosquitoes; fortunately, this problem is fairly easily resolved. After the mosquitoes lay their eggs, it takes a few days for the next generation to emerge. Knowing that, we can outfox them. If you're keeping a small basin of water or a birdbath out for the birds, just change the water in it every few days. If you have a pond that is too large to regularly change the water and you don't have a way to keep the water moving, then add some fish—there is nothing a healthy goldfish likes better than a few fat mosquito larvae for lunch.

Nesting opportunities

Do you live out in the country or in a very leafy suburb with plenty of natural nesting possibilities for birds? Trees with large forks in the branches or

This young Barn Swallow was wheeling about a marshy area on my patch and paused just long enough to be photographed. Easy to see, these birds fly so fast that it is very hard to catch a good image of them.

holes in their limbs? Are there cavities in old garden sheds and bargeboards? If so, then your birds are probably going to be able to find places suitable for their nesting needs without your help. Most of us, however, are not so blessed, and so it is good to consider ways to help the birds find what they need. In the modern world we tend not to let buildings and trees develop cavities—we tidy and patch and mend.

You might consider installing nesting boxes in your bird garden. Generally, you should use no more than four small nest boxes per acre for any one species. Put about 100 yards between bluebird boxes and 75 yards between swallow boxes (if you are fortunate enough to have both species, you can "pair" the houses, with one bluebird box 15 to 25 feet from a swallow box. Don't put bird houses near your feeders; don't put more than one box in a single tree, unless the tree is extremely large or the boxes are for different species. If you have very hot summers, you want to mount your boxes with the entrance holes facing north or east to prevent the boxes from overheating. Lastly, get the height right—many birds are very specific about the heights at which they will consider for setting up a nest. The internet is an excellent source of information about what specific birds are looking for in terms of nest box design and placement.

Plants at three levels

This means that your bird garden should have the following planting zones:

Ground cover. Low plants, perhaps in a herbaceous border, fairly closely spaced, in which birds that seek food on or near the ground can find both shelter and a plentiful supply of food, both plant and insect. Sadly, such parts of the garden also provide hiding and stalking opportunities for cats—so if you have a cat of your own, don't let it out to wander.

Ground cover does not comprise simply flowers. It also includes rocks and logs and piles of stones. In fact such features are essential, as they hold food. You should also leave piles of leaves and twigs in your garden, especially during the winter.

Shrubs and bushes. These, of course, are a source of food such as berries, seeds, and insects, but also provide a vantage point from which birds can look around to make sure it is safe, a perch to sing from and declaim "this is my territory," and shelter from predators and the weather. The shrubs and bush (intermediate) layer can be beautiful to look at. Ideally, it can contain species that start the year covered in flowers and then end it groaning under a crop of berries—some of which you might even get to eat yourself.

Higher trees. Such plants provide all of the features discussed above for those species that prefer a higher view of the world, as well as places for nest building. For the higher-tree layer you can be as adventurous as you wish, but

Three layers of planting: tall trees, shrubs, and ground cover.

as far as the birds are concerned, regular conifers and mixed deciduous trees are what they are looking for. Dense trees like cedars will be especially important in the winter.

Plant some of these trees right away once you have fixed on an overall design for you land—even small, young trees will improve the attractiveness of your garden to birds and over the years to come will mature into beautiful trees. Deciding where the trees will stand should be the first thing to fix on and then you can decide later on the details of the more complex decisions as to what shrubs and flowers will fill in the rest of the space.

If you already have trees on your land then don't be in too much of a rush to cut and trim them unless there is a serious safety problem. Even dead and dying trees can be attractive in their own right to us—and are immensely attractive to birds. They have really rich insect populations and can contain holes and hollows that many cavity-dwelling birds will be able to use for nesting and for shelter.

At the lowest level of planting there is the herbaceous border and, believe it or not, the lawn. Despite everything I've said about the importance of healthy clutter, there is no need for you to give up your lawn to have a bird garden. True, birds won't visit your garden if they don't feel safe, and the wide open spaces with few places to retreat to that look so great in the glossy magazines terrify many birds, who know that there are a lot of things out there just itching to eat them. But there are other species of birds that are actually adapted to open territories. Robins and flickers, for example, rather like grass—so do juncos and the odd sparrow. So some grass is fine, as long as it's not too much. Don't cut your lawn shorter than necessary. If you wish to have (or if your non-birding partner wishes to have) an even lawn then make sure to use a mulching mower that leaves the finely chopped clippings behind to nourish the soil and set the mower blades high so that you don't cut the grass to within an inch of its life. Not only will the grass actually survive dry spells better if left an inch or two longer than usual, but the available insect and seed food within the grass will be much richer in variety and quantity.

Scruffy corners

I know that for the majority of gardeners, having what I call a "scruffy corner" is anathema. Nevertheless, scruffy corners are highly desirable features of a wildlife or bird garden. Don't be too tidy in the fall—a clean garden with no leaf litter is a bad idea if you want to keep your birds and, for reasons that I will come to, is not good for the plants either. Take a deep breath and relax. The time to tidy your garden is the spring, not just before winter arrives. Scruffy corners provide food, shelter, and even reproductive opportunities for a lot of wildlife.

A log pile in a scruffy corner provides food and shelter.

Mixed plantings for birds can still be attractive to people.

Plenty of animals make their homes in dead wood and use it as a source of food. In natural woodlands, fallen wood occurs as a process of normal seasonal cycles, and many species have evolved and adapted to use this habitat. But in our increasingly tidy countryside, fallen and dead wood is not so common these days. Even out in your wider birding patch you will undoubtedly have noticed that within days of a storm bringing down branches they are often cleared away and tidied up by somebody who is unaware of the harm this does to the wildlife.

A pile of logs in a quiet corner of your garden simulates fallen trees and is essential in an effective wildlife garden. Even in the smallest backyard, you should be able to find somewhere to put a pile of logs. They are best placed in a shady spot, so that they remain cool and damp. The Victorians not only had rockeries, they also had "stumperies"—so if your partner complains or your neighbor looks askance at your designs, simply explain that you are gardening in the Victorian style and they will be so impressed they may even try to copy you. A log pile can be as simple as . . . a pile of logs. Or it can be an elaborate architectural wonder. Just make sure it has some fresh wood, some rotting wood, and plenty of loose bark. Build your piles of logs, perhaps intermixed with some rocks, into stacks using pretty much anything on hand and then leave them to be colonized by insects and fungi. The birds and other beasts, some of them destined to be bird food, will love you for it. And these stumperies do, you will have to admit, look interesting.

Achieving the sort of scruffiness that birds like is not something that comes easily to neat-minded people, but it is well worth it. Leave a corner of your flower beds unraked in the fall; pile up some logs and rocks; leave the heads of seed-bearing flowers uncut before winter. Then pour yourself a drink and relax while the birds settle into your bird garden.

WHAT PLANTS SHOULD I HAVE?

This is the crux of the business. The following paragraphs suggest some good-looking, easy-to-grow plants that will be exactly what the birds are looking for. I live in Quebec, one of the damper, more northerly parts of the continent, and these plants are ones that I know will work well in similar climatic zones. However, if you are designing your bird garden in a hotter and dryer area, just make a note of the plant types and groups mentioned here, as there are many hot-climate equivalents. It's the principles that matter rather than the specifics.

There are seven main groups of plants to consider when planning your bird garden. The suggestions that follow are based, among other sources, on materials originally released by the excellent people at the Cornell Laboratory of Ornithology; you can learn more by visiting their website, www.birds.cornell.edu.

Conifers

Evergreen trees and shrubs, such as pines, spruces, firs, arborvitae, and junipers, provide excellent shelter, nest sites, and food for many species. Some northern finches specialize in extracting seeds from conifer cones, and some hummingbirds take insects and sap from the tips of conifer branches when they first return in spring, before nectar-bearing flowers are available. Really good candidates for a bird garden are spruces and the several varieties of juniper, from the low and ground-hugging plants to the tall, treelike forms. These plants have a dense covering of needlelike leaves and produce a heavy crop of fruits for birds to eat. They give excellent shelter from weather and predators and plenty of insects can be found within their close-packed branches. Junipers are also attractive plants that look fine in any garden—they please the eye of the gardener as well as the wildlife.

Grasses and leguminacae

Grasslands and smaller stands of grasses and "weeds" provide cover for ground-nesting birds. They also provide abundant food for many species. Note, though, that they can serve as deathtraps if you mow them during the nesting season, should your plot be extensive enough to harbor any of the few species that makes nests on the ground, such as Bobolinks. It's always a good principle anyway not to cut your grass too short. Let it grow a bit and maybe even allow some corners to set seed. Some grouped plantings of the large, specialist grasses, native or foreign, will look attractive and provide foraging for certain bird species.

Flowers that contain good supplies of nectar

Flowers, especially those with tubular red corollas such as monarda, attract hummingbirds and orioles. The insects attracted to these plants also serve as food for a wide variety of birds. You and birds will enjoy any of the following species: coneflowers, sunflowers, zinnias, black-eyed Susan, monarda, buddleia, goldenrod, Joe-Pye weed, milkweed, and asters.

Summer-fruiting plants

This includes various species of cherry, chokecherry, native honeysuckle, raspberry, serviceberry, blackberry, blueberry, native mulberry, and elderberry. These all provide food for many birds during the breeding season.

Fall-fruiting plants

Dogwoods, mountain ash, cotoneasters, buffalo-berries, and other fall-bearing fruit and berry plants provide an important source of food for migratory birds, both to build up fat reserves before migration and sustain them along their journey. Non-migratory birds also fatten up on these so they can start the winter in good physical condition. Viburnums are a very good choice and their berries are bright and attractive in the winter, but make sure to plant native species, which birds like, and not breeders' cultivated varieties, many of which have become unappetizing to birds.

Plants that keep (some) fruit in winter

Some plants hold onto their fruits long after they ripen in the fall. These essential plants provide a food source for winter residents and early returning migrants. Robins, waxwings, Pine Grosbeaks, and Northern Mockingbirds are among the birds drawn to fruit trees in winter. Crabapple, snowberry, native bittersweet, sumacs, viburnums, American highbush cranberry, eastern wahoo, Virginia creeper, and winterberry (holly) are all valuable for these birds.

Trees that produce nuts

Nuts are a very rich and sustaining food source for those birds with the ability to get at their contents. They are also very attractive in their own right and will look good in any garden design. Suitable trees and shrubs include oaks, hickories, buckeyes, chestnuts, butternuts, walnuts, beeches, and hazels. These will provide food for birds such as titmice, jays, Wild Turkeys, woodpeckers, and other "mast-eaters"; insects drawn to the spring flowers of these plants provide abundant food to fuel spring migration. It is also worth noting that these and other trees also provide nesting habitat for many species.

I hope you have a lot of fun and pleasure creating your green birding garden—and then even more pleasure adding new and interesting birds to your green birding list.

"Saturday was the first time I've ever done a walking BIGBY Christmas Bird Count. Here are my three favorite birds from my Christmas Bird Count along Milwaukee's lakefront:

"My first favorite bird was a big surprise. I'd barely left home and was walking down the ramp that heads down the lake bluff from the intersection of Prospect and Ogden. At the top of the ramp I heard some crows doing some serious mobbing. I stopped halfway down the ramp and saw the crows gathered in a wooded area along the bluff, not too far from the ramp. Following the direction the crows were all looking, I spotted a magnificent GREAT HORNED OWL maybe 50 feet away from me! Well camouflaged. I would never have seen it if the crows hadn't pointed it out to me. The owl seemed completely unperturbed by the unwelcome attention it was receiving from the crows. Maybe only the second or third time I've seen a Great Horned Owl in broad daylight. Really made my day! Only one block away from home, and MilWALKee BIGBY species #192 for 2010.

"My second CBC favorite bird was pretty cool. Eastern Meadowlark in Lakeshore State Park. Had to look around quite a bit to find it in the small prairie there. I'd seen the bird only once over the past week, but got a quick glimpse on Saturday. Two other people had seen it as well earlier this week. My gut says "Eastern Meadowlark." But I'm reporting the bird as "Meadowlark species" on the CBC because I didn't have long enough looks to completely rule out Western Meadowlark. I have one blurred photo of the bird in flight, in poor lighting (taken by someone else). I've shown it to a number of other folks, and the consensus is that yes, it's definitely a Meadowlark. But none of them could conclude Eastern or Western from the photo.

"And my third favorite CBC bird was the old reliable dependable female Long-tailed Duck in Lakeshore State Park. I've seen it every day the past week or so. Good close-up views! At least two birders have posted great photos of the bird. When I last saw it Saturday, it was in the patch of open water under the footbridge to Lakeshore State Park. It spent most of its time underwater, surfacing to catch its breath and then diving again. I found myself hoping that it was finding sufficient food on its frequent dives . . .

"Very cold day to be out birding, but very satisfying!!"

—Bernie Sloan, http://bird-bs.blogspot.com

Citizen Science

7

You will have gathered by now that, although green birding started among the ranks of the more competitive listers, it has the potential to involve you in much more than simply getting the longest list with the lowest carbon footprint. Green birding is just as much, if not more so, about getting to know the birds in your locality on a deeper level—something that begs the question of what to do with all that knowledge you've accumulated.

Since the earliest days of birding, amateur ornithologists have been immensely important observers and recorders of bird population changes and bird behaviors, and many have contributed greatly to the science of ornithology. In other fields, amateur botanists and lepidopterists, for example, have made similarly important scientific contributions, but no group has done as much to aid the academic community as the birders of the world. Green birders can add our pieces to the great puzzle of avian science by concentrating on our local bird communities in greater depth.

Never think that your observations have no use to the wider world or no meaning to anyone other than yourself. All of our individual contributions and observations, brought together, help build a better understanding of the lives of birds. They are the vital building blocks from which the scientific corpus of ornithology is built. Without the enormous amounts of data that are collected and submitted by birding citizen scientists our knowledge would be meager indeed.

There are a number of formal, organized citizen science projects that you can participate in while green birding. For the most part, these projects are relatively easy to join, have a well-organized means of submitting your observations, and will give you ample feedback on the submissions of others and how they all tie together with yours.

"Over there—in the reeds." If you see a group of birders looking intently at something, make sure to check out what is attracting their attention.

WHAT IS CITIZEN SCIENCE?

Citizen Science is a term that has arisen to describe a number of large scientific projects that involve multiple observers in widespread locations, often with little or no formal scientific training, performing research activities that involve observation, measurement, calculation, and deduction.

Using the data gathered by these citizen scientists, professional ornithologists are able to perform research projects that otherwise, usually because of the vast amounts of data needed, would be impossible or at least very difficult and expensive to conduct. In addition, there is a considerable educational benefit to the birders contributing to these projects, and both the amateur and professional birding worlds profit from the increased cooperation and engagement between the two worlds.

Many citizen science projects run over long periods of annual and seasonal data collection. The majority are focused on gathering information about bird populations and activity that is essential to the study of changes in bird populations, migration routes, breeding success, and the interaction between birds and their habitats. This is important, not only because of the intrinsic interest of this knowledge, but also because without this knowledge effective resource management cannot take place.

We can all use our local patches or even our gardens as the laboratories in which we perform citizen science. Participating in these projects is interesting and fulfilling and will keep us engaged for years to come, knowing that what we are doing has a wider utility than simply providing us with a hobby.

PROJECTS YOU CAN CONTRIBUTE TO

There are a wide selection of formal citizen science projects that are easy and enjoyable to take part in. All of the ones described in this section are organized by reputable organizations, universities, wildlife charities, and specialized research groups; the biggest ones in North America are those coordinated by the Audubon Society and the Cornell Laboratory of Ornithology. Some projects are ones that you can contribute to whenever and wherever you go out birding, while others are site- or season-specific and may only ask you to gather data for relatively short periods each year.

eBird

We have already mentioned this fantastic project elsewhere as it is a primary means of sharing the bird sightings that you make on your patch and local birding routes. eBird is the simplest of all the citizen science projects to take part in and undoubtedly the most important. It runs 365 days a year and is totally applicable to the localized data collection of the green birder working his or her patch and local trails.

The program has been running since 2002 and is managed by the Cornell Laboratory and National Audubon Society in the U.S. and by Bird Studies Canada north of the border. Birders who contribute to it can keep track of their own sightings while simultaneously creating a massive collection of bird sightings worldwide. Millions and millions of observations are recorded each year, and the number is growing almost exponentially. Although this began as a North American project, it is now possible to enter bird data from anywhere on the planet, thus making the database truly universal in scope and achievement.

The project asks birders to report the birds they observe and compiles the results to create a picture of bird distribution and populations. A simple web interface allows you to submit your observations online: after each birding session, you go to the website and enter when, where, and how you went birding and then report all the birds you saw or heard during the outing. All submissions are reviewed by a data filter to catch unusual sightings that might be entry or identification errors, which are then verified by local bird experts.

In addition, eBird provides online tools that allow you to view your personal records as well as compiled eBird data, with interactive maps and graphs. You can do all of this in English, Spanish, and French.

The data collected by eBird is used by ornithologists at Cornell and other universities in their various research projects. It is also passed along to other databases such as the Avian Knowledge Network (AKN) and the international Global Biodiversity Information Facility (GBIF).

Most birders only get two chances a year to see White-crowned Sparrows as they pass through in migration; except in the West, their breeding territory is very far north. Their call is distinctive, however, and they are easily spotted when they are in the area.

Priority Migrant eBird

Priority Migrant eBird is a program that focuses on data collection for five species of birds that migrate to winter in Central and South America: the Cerulean, Golden-winged, Blue-winged, and Canada Warblers and the Olive-sided Flycatcher. This project asks participants to report sightings (including species and numbers of individual birds, where and when seen, and other relevant information such as the weather) of non-breeding birds in order to collect the data needed to develop effective conservation strategies for these and other long-distance migratory species that have experienced recent population declines. Participants use the familiar eBird online platform to submit data. The species studied in this project are somewhat scarce and you may not have them on your patch—but if you do and you believe that your skills of observation are up to the task, why not make your contribution? This project is important for the futures of these and other species.

Christmas Bird Counts

Christmas Bird Counts, organized by the Audubon Society, are perhaps the oldest citizen science projects of all, dating back to the early 1900s. You may have already participated in one; if not, you have a treat in store. These annual events attract many birders of all levels of experience, get you out in the open air in an excellent cause, and almost always include a party at the end of the day where you can meet other birders and socialize while the results are tabulated by the local count compilers.

CBCs are exhaustive bird population counts carried out on a single day in mid to late December. The goal is to count all the birds in a 15-mile circle around a certain point and inevitably requires a lot of birders to be done properly—these are certainly not projects that you could do alone. If there is a CBC circle in your area and if you can access it without your car, then you can to do a Green CBC count. Contact the organizer of your local count and offer your services—as an experienced birder, you will probably be snapped up and assigned a route to check.

There are hundreds of such counts every year and so there is a good chance that there is one near where you live. The data from each of the count areas is sent to Audubon for final compilation and then, in conjunction with the counts from earlier years, enables scientists and birders like you to develop a picture of bird populations over the entire continent. This sort of information is important for such purposes as looking for increases or, more often these days, decreases in the numbers of birds in general or of particular species in a given region. Having data collected over such a long time and according to the same protocol each year is hugely valuable and important. There is nothing else comparable.

Project FeederWatch

FeederWatch is another citizen science project with a long history. This one is tailor-made for the green birder, as you do it in your own backyard and can count all your birds from the warmth and comfort of an armchair—an important factor when you consider that this is a winter project and parts of this continent get mighty cold.

During the FeederWatch period, participants are asked to count the birds that come within the vicinity of their garden feeders. You do this on two consecutive days per week during the winter months. You are not required to spend all your time on those days watching for birds, just to note how many hours you kept an eye open for visiting birds.

Each week, you enter your numbers into an online form like the eBird form. You will be able to see how your numbers build up over the season, compare the current year to previous years, and also compare your sightings to those of other FeederWatchers, wherever they may be.

The Great Backyard Bird Count

The GBBC is rather similar to Project FeederWatch, except that it is done over a single long weekend in February and you do not have to confine yourself to

Counting the birds that visit your feeder is easy to do, and it provides important data to scientists and conservationists.

your garden feeders. Counts in the GBBC can be done anywhere and for as long or as short a time as you can manage—so you could do the count on one of your regular birding routes, on your patch, or wherever you think good birds are to be seen. This project gathers a detailed snapshot of bird distribution in mid-winter and is enormously valuable.

NestWatch

If you have nesting boxes on your property or on your patch, or you know of someone who has boxes, you can contribute to this project.

NestWatch organizers supply tips and plans for providing safe housing for bluebirds, swallows, chickadees, and other cavity-nesting birds at their resource center; to participate, you register the boxes you will be monitoring on the website and then report your observations of which birds used the boxes, when they used them, how many eggs were laid, and how many birds fledged. Your data will be used by scientists to learn more about nesting birds and how climate change is affecting them.

Birds in Forested Landscapes

This is a more difficult and advanced project, but one of immense interest and usefulness. If your patch includes a forested area, however fragmented, then you might consider joining the project.

Birds in Forested Landscapes studies the habitat and conservation needs of forest-dwelling birds throughout North America. The project attempts to answer many questions about the way habitat changes are affecting high-priority species of forest-dwelling birds, focusing on gaps in scientific knowledge: What size of habitat do these birds need? How much fragmentation will they tolerate? How do they respond to various land use practices? Conservationists use the data collected to understand the habitat needs of forest birds of special concern and develop conservation strategies to sustain their populations.

Citizen scientists like you are asked to collect data that answers particular questions about birds in your forest patch. There is quite a lot of flexibility in what you will be asked to do because this project aims to connect professional scientists with many different research projects with birders in the field who can help them gather more data than they could by themselves. There is plenty of information at www.birds.cornell.edu/bfl.

BFL can be used to study almost any forest bird species and the habitats they depend upon. For example, one very successful project looked at the effects of forest fragmentation and climate change on continent-wide populations of tanagers. To a great extent you will be able to pick and choose the projects that are relevant to your patch and that you feel you have the skills and interest to participate in.

Canadian Loon Lake Survey

As the title indicates, this is a project that is run in Canada; green birders who happen to have a lake on their patch that may hold loons in the summer months will be able to participate. If you can take part in this study, you are doubly blessed—being a Canadian with a loon lake is one of life's great joys!

This is a long-term project designed to monitor the numbers and breeding success of loons on lakes across Canada. The ultimate objective is to preserve loons by increasing our understanding of the species and of human impact on them.

Participants are asked to survey a lake at least three times over the summer: in June to watch for pairs of loons occupying the lake; in July to look for newly-hatched chicks; and in August to record the number of chicks that have survived the summer.

You will be provided with a survey kit and detailed instructions that tell you exactly what to do. You are free to decide which lake(s) you wish to survey; even lakes without loons provide valuable information, since it is helpful to determine what factors might exclude loons from an area. The survey includes a questionnaire that will allow the project to assess factors affecting the breeding success of loons in Canada, including the effects of water-level changes, artificial nesting platforms, and recreational use of personal watercraft.

Many survey volunteers contribute to loon conservation in other ways as well. You can take water samples from lakes, submit loon carcasses and unhatched eggs for analysis, post educational signs provided by the survey, or make floating nest platforms (the survey distributes plans for building these).

The survey's results appear regularly in *BirdWatch Canada,* the newsletter of Bird Studies Canada.

The Marsh Monitoring Program

The Marsh Monitoring Program (MMP) is a long-term program that works to understand and conserve wetlands and their inhabitants (amphibians and birds) across the Great Lakes basin. The MMP is run jointly by Bird Studies Canada and Environment Canada, the Great Lakes Commission, Environment Canada-Ontario Region, and the U.S. Environmental Protection Agency.

The project does not simply concern itself with birds but also allows you to look at amphibian and other marsh-dwelling species. If you live near an area of marsh in the Great Lakes basin that you can reach by the usual self-powered means, then you can probably contribute to our understanding of this particularly susceptible habitat and the birds who live in it through this study. Participants provide information about the size, area, drainage, plant species, water levels, and so on of their chosen marsh and then at specified times of the year, mostly during the breeding season, conduct surveys of the species of birds present and what they are doing. To help with this, you will be provided with training materials and detailed protocols to make sure that you collect you data in a standardized manner. You might also be asked to help monitor frogs and toads.

If you do not live in the Great Lakes area but have an accessible area of marshland, then the ideas and procedures of this project could well be the basis of an independent survey you could conduct on your own. We'll talk more about independent projects in chapter 8.

Nocturnal owl surveys

Bird Studies Canada conducts nocturnal owl surveys all over the country. Birders taking part in these type of surveys use recorded Boreal and Barred Owl calls to encourage owls to call in response. Participants are given a route consisting of 10 stops positioned 2 kilometers apart (a quite cyclable distance) and are asked to survey their route during one evening in April, making note of all owls heard or seen.

Although this type of formal, organized surveys seem mostly to be confined on a large scale to Canada, the methods used are commonly adopted by birders all over the continent, and you or your friends in a local birding club could easily adopt these procedures. It is not at all difficult and you will probably be quite surprised at just how many owls are living around you if you go out looking for them in this fashion. Just one more means to keep an eye and an ear on your patch.

WHAT HAS CITIZEN SCIENCE ACHIEVED?

The data collected by birders acting on their own or with others in citizen science projects is immensely important—central even—to ornithological science. Without these contributions many pivotal studies could never have been conducted. A lot of important information about birds, their habitats, and changes in bird populations has been published directly as a result of the data gathered by citizen scientists. Some examples are listed here.

- Data collected by the Birds in Forested Landscapes project and a variety of Breeding Bird Surveys was used in establishing that acid rain has a negative effect on the ability of Wood Thrushes to successfully nest and raise their young. The general effect of acid rain on a range of other species has been reported in a number of similar papers. (Hames et al. 2002)
- In the United Kingdom and many other developed countries, there have been huge increases in the amount of intensive agriculture compared to more traditional methods of farming. The British Trust for

Ornithology Common Birds Census, a citizen science project, helped scientists demonstrate that this change in farming practices has contributed significantly to declines in populations of many species of birds.

- From analysis of fifty-seven years of citizen scientist data, the British Trust for Ornithology's Nest Record Scheme has been able to show that the date on which the vast majority of birds lay their eggs is related to temperature or rainfall. Green birders will not be surprised to learn that long-term trends clearly indicate that climate change is an important factor in the changes in egg-laying behavior and nesting success that this study has observed in recent years.

- The Cornell Laboratory of Ornithology's North American Nest Record Card Program, together with five comparable nest record programs in Canada, has shown that Tree Swallows are now laying their eggs on average nine days earlier than they were thirty years ago. There is strong evidence that this is associated with climate change.

- House Finches are very susceptible to eye diseases, so much so that the numbers of House Finches in different regions is linked to the prevalence of disease in those regions. It has been estimated that a conjunctivitis caused by the bacterium *Mycoplasma gallisepticum* has decreased the population of this species by some 180 million birds. The organism that causes the disease is common in poultry and is thought to have spread from farms to wild birds sometime in the past twenty or so years. Humans are not affected. Data collected by participants of the House Finch Disease Survey, FeederWatch, and the continent-wide annual Christmas Bird Counts has been central to the study of this situation.

- Several studies have looked at how bird populations change in distribution over time. Data submitted by birders has helped to show that breeding success of many species of birds is affected by environmental changes. As our climate changes, the availability of suitable foods, especially within the short breeding season, is showing signs of getting out of alignment with the needs of birds, hampering the ability of parent birds to adequately raise their young.

I could go on, but by now you likely get the idea. The data that you will gather by pursuing citizen science projects on your local patch help scientists

Walking birders communing with a Barred Owl. This bird had been sitting out in the open for some hours on a cold January day but almost nobody walking past was aware of it. Look up and keep your eyes open.

and the government departments develop environmental and land-use policies, and look after birds and the places where they live. Never forget that, as the expert on the wildlife and birds of your local patch, you are probably the person best placed to gather the information over a period of months and years that underpins these important research projects. Citizen science performed by regular birders like you plays an essential role in the study and conservation of birds.

Personal Research in Your Patch

8

Once you have got a taste for simple scientific investigations through your experiences with citizen science projects (and almost all birders do put their toes in this water at some point), you may well find yourself wondering what else you can do on your own birding patch.

Inevitably, as you have walked and cycled the trails around your home, you will have observed things that triggered questions in your mind. Surely those cardinals have not raised *three* broods of young this season? I am suddenly seeing Indigo Buntings where I never saw them before—what has happened to attract them? When do the first Tree Swallows arrive in spring and leave in the fall—and are the dates shifting over the years? What is the preferred food of "my" American Robins and does it change much as the young leave the nest?

Population growth in our large urban communities and the inevitable contributions it makes to pollution, habitat destruction, and greenhouse gas emissions is a serious problem if we are concerned for the continuing health of our bird populations. While there are some species of birds that do appear to benefit from the urban environment—starlings and crows, for example, find great opportunities for food scavenging near our homes and factories—most species are negatively affected by towns and cities. In more rural surroundings, the impacts of human activity on birds may be no less severe—and in many cases even more so, as agricultural activity ploughs up rich grasslands, forests are logged and fragmented, and new roads and other developments break up important habitats into smaller and less bird-friendly plots, to say nothing of the effects of industrial and agricultural pollution.

The question is, how do we actually measure these impacts in a meaningful manner so that policy makers can have the information they need to mitigate the damage? Politicians need sound data; they cannot (although sadly, they all too often do) rely on anecdotal evidence. But at the same time they tend not to employ specialists who can gather the data they need. Hence, the value of the observations that come from citizen scientists like you.

This section of the book will present you with some typical questions that most birders ask themselves as they become more familiar with a particular piece of habitat and will offer you some suggestions as to how to try to find the answers. Often, and surprisingly, you will discover that nobody actually knows the answer; when you work out what is going on you will, in your own small way, have added something to the extensive corpus of ornithological knowledge. The great thing about amateur birders is that we have the time to spend on investigating the small and obscure questions that the professionals do not have the oppportunity or the funding to pursue but which are interesting nevertheless.

Birders coming to patch birding from the listing end of the game sometimes underestimate their own abilities to contribute to ornithological studies because they are not "scientists." Not true! If we go about finding the answers to our questions in a methodical manner then we are all scientists. With care, anyone can devise a way to study something that interests them; we can speculate, form hypotheses, and look for evidence to confirm or disprove our hypotheses. That is the basis of the scientific method and all of us can make use of it.

There are three basic questions we can ask about bird populations:

- Which species are to be seen on my patch? (inventory)
- How many of each species are on my patch? (abundance)
- How successful are they at what they do—raising young and so on? (behavior)

Let's look at these questions—and how you can investigate them—in greater depth. I am going to suggest some approaches that green birders can take to these questions: simple, basic ways to answer them as well as some more complex solutions. I'll also introduce you to a technique known as point counting; this is fairly advanced, and for birders who are still learning their craft it may be something to return to later. Nevertheless, this is an important method to learn because it answers these census questions most effectively.

INVENTORY: WHICH BIRD SPECIES
ARE TO BE SEEN ON MY PATCH?

The simplest way to answer this is really not much more than an extension of what birders do all the time. You go out to your patch, walk or cycle your local trails and roads, and make a note of what you see.

Of course, you want to be able to compare your bird list season to season and year to year and so it is always important to ensure that you at least record the date and time of day on which you made your observations, but as

Don't grumble about American Crows. They may be common, but not many species are more interesting.

a listing birder you probably do that anyway. Actually, this sort of very basic bird counting is the essence of listing and almost every birder, green or otherwise, engages in this activity. Thus, at rock bottom, every birder is an active observational scientist.

It is good to have a copy of a checklist for your area so that you know what could or should be present at some time of each year. Why? Because the *absence* of a bird is almost as important as the presence of one. Local checklists can be obtained from guidebooks and the internet and via your local birding club or society.

A good example of this point is the ubiquitous House Sparrow (*Passer domesticus*). This bird has lived alongside people and human habitations for some 7,000 or more years—since the very earliest days of agriculture and the establishment of stable settlements in the Middle East. Humans have always taken the presence of "sparrows" for granted, part of the background noise, as it were and many birders got into the habit of not even noting them. To some these were the ultimate "trash birds." But then, one day, we started to realize that they were not as ubiquitous as they had been, that we were seeing less of them and that, in fact, in some places where they used to be common we were not seeing them at all. A lot of research has been done in recent years to try to determine the reasons for this reduction in the population of such a universally loved/hated little brown bird, and we are gradually beginning to work out what is going on and why. But that work has been hampered by the fact that for the most part House Sparrows were simply ignored by birders—so while we could say "there used to be a lot more of them" we did not have the historical data to back up that observation or to enable us to start figuring out why they are now less common.

Negative data is just as important as positive data and so, as you wander your patch, make sure to take note of the birds that *ought* to be present (but aren't) as well as the ones that actually are. By so doing you might be one of the first people to notice the silence of the canary in the mine shaft and may be able to alert the world to an environmental problem that can be fixed before it gets out of hand.

Although we all like to wander off the beaten track and will be distracted by the call of an unusual or unknown bird away in the distance, try to keep some regularity to the routes you follow so that the data that you collect is reasonably standardized in the way it was gathered.

That is the essence of a basic bird inventory—which, as a lister, you were effectively doing anyway.

ABUNDANCE: HOW MANY BIRDS LIVE ON MY PATCH AND WHERE ARE THEY?

This is about adding numbers to our lists and is always an interesting question—both to us as individual birders, but also to ornithologists. Most serious bird surveys involve some degree of abundance assessment, and if you repeat such measurements over long periods of time, you will have an excellent way to discover long-term changes or trends in the populations of particular birds.

Which species are increasing in number and which are decreasing? Is there an association between the two? What outside factors might be having an effect—is climate change causing southerly birds to move north, for example, or is pollution affecting the availability of food? Are new predators appearing on your patch (cats, perhaps from a nearby housing development)? An abundance count, repeated over time, will help you find some of the answers to those questions.

The simplest approach to this, and a surprisingly robust one, is to take the method you used for determining which species are present (the listing procedure) and simply add an estimate of the numbers of individual birds you come across during each outing, both seen and heard. Take care not to double count any birds; after all, they have a habit of moving about a lot. Again, remember to report your data to eBird, who love to have numbers if you have them.

An easy way to ensure that you don't double count is to make at least some of your observations at specific and repeatable points on your route. The points should be spaced apart enough to make sure the birds you see or hear at one point are not the same ones you count a few yards down the trail. If you are trying to add this degree of control into your procedure then you are well on the way to performing a full point count census of your patch, something that is described in detail later in this chapter.

BEHAVIOR: HOW SUCCESSFUL ARE "MY" BIRDS AND ARE THEY RAISING YOUNG AS THEY SHOULD?

If you are asking this question, you are about to embark on the fascinating world of the breeding bird survey (BBS). A BBS is a formalized means of determining which birds are not just passing through your patch but are actually resident, paired off, and nesting. Because birds move around a lot, the less territorial ones may visit your area because the food is plentiful and later move elsewhere as conditions and seasons change—but they all have a "base" somewhere. For instance, you might have two hundred robins that spend time on your patch, but only fifty have nests there. A BBS can help reveal this kind of information.

At this time, you might like to ask about your local birding community and see if there is an "atlasing" project under way; if so, the organizers would love to have your information to add to their database. Atlasing is the name we give to the collection of information about bird presence and breeding activity for the eventual production of a breeding bird atlas for a particular area. Typically, an atlas of breeding birds is an enormous body of work that is ideally reproduced about every twenty years. It involves considerable resources and large teams of amateur and professional birders over a four- or five-year data collection period. If there is no such effort in your state or province, then what you learn while doing your own patch survey will stand you in good stead when one does start up—as it surely will one day.

Some of the procedures that are used to provide the answers to this question are beyond the scope of amateur birders; such studies may involve mist-netting and banding, which nobody is allowed to do without a long apprenticeship and a license showing that they are competent. Nevertheless, banding stations almost always depend on enthusiastic volunteer birders to help with various tasks that make the banding possible and will often provide training opportunities for those who show interest and aptitude. If you're interested in participating in this kind of study, see if there's a banding station near you.

But what about your own site? Probably there is no atlas project happening this year and no banding station within reach of your stout boots and cycle. Let's assume that you simply want to unveil the breeding and success status of the birds that you have been counting on your own personal patch for your own interest.

First of all, you will be relieved to learn that you don't have to find all of the birds' nests in order to determine how many and which species are

It is a great treat to find nests on your patch, close enough to home that you can follow the birds' development over the days and weeks. This juvenile Blue Jay was frequently seen in my garden, begging food from its parents by shivering its wings.

successfully breeding. Actually, the chances are that you wouldn't find many nests anyway; birds are simply very good at being birds, and to be successful they need to hide their nests in places that predators will not be able to discover. If you do find a nest, be careful not to approach it too closely if it is occupied, and make sure that others do not learn of its location from you. Make a note and then back off and leave the birds alone.

To investigate your birds' breeding success, you will look for evidence of "breeding activity" and from that try to deduce the presence of actively nesting birds. It takes a careful eye and ear and some care and concentration to decide which birds are breeding nearby, which might be, and which probably are—but it is not difficult if you are organized. The signs to look for in the following paragraphs are a simplified selection of those used by atlasers, but they are more than sufficient for a survey of your local patch. As the season progresses, you will usually be able to move certain birds from the "possibly" to the "probably" to the "definitely" breeding categories, while others will remain stuck at a lower level because you cannot get that final clinching piece of evidence.

Look for, and write down:

Birds that are almost certainly not breeding. This would include any species you saw during the breeding season which was not in its appropriate breeding habitat and for which you really have no evidence that it is breeding anywhere in the vicinity. For example, several species of male ducks or gulls disperse from their breeding territory after eggs have been laid and can be found almost anywhere, even though it is still their breeding period. Other examples might be species for which there is an overlap between migrants and breeders and you cannot tell which is which simply by looking at them.

Almost in the same category are those **birds that are possibly, but probably not, breeding.** These would be birds that you see on your patch in suitable breeding habitat during their breeding season but for which you have no other evidence that they actually are breeding. Maybe they are juveniles that have not found mates or migrants that are still passing through or simply they are just being very discrete about their activities.

Then we have **birds that are possibly or probably breeding.** Signs of possible breeding include a bird that is heard singing or drumming in suitable habitat during its breeding season. You will need to look for further evidence (see below) to back up birds that you place in this category. These are birds of interest that you will want to follow more closely to see if they give more definite signs of breeding activity.

Birds that are very probably breeding on your patch are not that difficult to assess if you look for the right pieces of evidence. There are several marker activities that would make you assign a bird to this category. These include:

- A number of birds in different locations producing sounds associated with breeding in suitable habitat
- A pair of birds seen in suitable habitat—this is easiest to note for species such as ducks or Northern Cardinals that have clear sexual dimorphism
- An adult bird seen on suitable breeding territory on at least two occasions, a week or more apart, during the breeding season
- A male and a female bird engaged in courtship displays or territorial disputes
- A bird visiting a suitable nesting site—usually this can only be said with confidence of cavity-nesting species
- Agitated behavior and/or alarm calls in suitable habitat
- A brood patch or cloacal protuberance observed on an adult in suitable habitat (not easy to see)

This Great Blue Heron is carrying nesting material in its beak—one of the signs to look out for if you are doing a breeding bird survey on your patch.

- Active nest building or nest hole excavation by species such as woodpeckers and wrens that prepare several nest sites but only use one or that go through the motions of nesting without actually laying eggs and hatching them.

Lastly, there are those **birds that you can be pretty confident are breeding.** You should look for:

- Birds carrying nest building materials, or any species other than wrens and woodpeckers actively building nests
- An adult bird trying to draw attention away from a nest or young birds
- An empty nest or the presence of shells of current-year eggs
- Obviously recently fledged juvenile birds incapable of sustained flight
- An adult entering or leaving a probable nesting site whose behavior is suggestive of an occupied nest
- An adult bird carrying a fecal sac
- An adult carrying food that would seem to be for feeding young
- A nest containing apparently viable eggs
- A nest containing one or more young (seen or heard)

In an atlas project, some common shorthand codes are assigned to these pieces of evidence and you might find this system helpful when making your own notes—check the internet for detailed information or get involved with your local bird atlasing group if there is one.

Armed with the data that you will assemble using the procedures listed here you will soon build up a pretty good idea of which species of birds are breeding or probably breeding on your patch. Repeating the survey over two or three years will make it all the more useful.

DEVELOPING A SIMPLE BIRD CENSUS PROJECT

You could think of this as being "scientific listing"—listing with a somewhat more detailed methodology. The paragraphs that follow describe a simple protocol that you (and your friends) can follow over the seasons and years ahead and thereby be able to build a really detailed picture of what the birds on your patch are up to.

First of all, decide whether you are going to do this study yourself, with a friend or family member, or with like-minded acquaintances from your local birding organization. Doing this sort of investigation with others is always a pleasure and will also allow your group to be able to gather data on days when you are ill or otherwise unavailable. Having someone with whom to share the work and pleasure will also encourage you to keep at it and complete the task.

It is very important, when doing scientifically meaningful surveys, that you be absolutely consistent with your methodology. Each time you go out to make observations you must do so in precisely the same manner as you do on other occasions; you must collect data at the same time of day and in the same places. Only by doing this can you draw conclusions and make comparisons over the seasons and years. You may not be a trained, professional scientist but what you are doing is still very real science—so don't cut corners.

Note that, for the protocol described here, you should be a moderately skilled observer. If you can identify the twenty-five most common local species quickly by sight or sound and are familiar with most other birds likely to be seen in the area (though you may need to quickly refer to a field guide for certain less-common or difficult-to-separate species), then you have the basic skills you need.

Objectives

- To gather and analyze information about the distribution and abundance of birds on your local patch and make that information available to the wider birding community.
- To try to associate your observations about bird populations with the nature of the habitat that you are surveying and use this to identify actual and potential problems.

Method

There are two ways to do this type of study. One (a good option if your time is limited) is to take a single snapshot of the bird population during peak breeding period each year; the other is to examine the situation throughout the year, making regular (for example, quarterly) observations in specific designated locations. You can do either type of study, or you can do both.

Through the snapshot census you will collect data during a fixed period each year from a number of related sites across the area in which you routinely enjoy your green birding. This will allow you to better understand the distribution of birds on your patch and to monitor year-to-year changes in the bird population of your locality. Through the longer seasonal surveys, you can collect year-round data at several bird-rich sites, thereby developing a more complete picture of all the bird species that occur on your patch and evaluate the importance of a varied selection of local habitats to birds.

The snapshot census

Your snapshot census should be done each year during the peak breeding period for birds in your area—probably sometime between late April and early June, depending on where you live.

Get a good map of your local area that includes your patch and the various routes that you walk and cycle when out birding. You should concern yourself with the area that you can reasonably expect to be able to cover by the self-powered means at your disposal. Add the information available from various online sources to your map; in particular, the satellite imaging at Google Earth will help you to identify all those hidden and potentially birdy corners that you could otherwise overlook.

Divide the area into a grid, with squares half a mile (1 kilometer) on each side.

In each square (or in as many as practical), decide on a route that you can walk or cycle or canoe. It might be along roads, following formal trails, or it could be a piece of bushwhacking. Routes can be linked across square boundaries, but if the trail you are following does cross into another square—as it likely will—then keep a separate collection of data for the portion of the trail in the new square. That is to say, when your trail crosses a square boundary, you will think of it as starting a new survey route.

On each of these routes select six to ten survey points. Ideally these points should be selected at random—not because you think they will have a particularly high probability of being in good, bird-rich habitat. It is just as important to discover where the birds are not as to find out where they are. There are a number of mathematically acceptable methods for taking the bias out of your selection but for practical purposes, you could as well ask a friend who is not taking part in your survey to stick ten pins in the map random distances apart—the important thing is to not allow bias to come into the selection of the points. The other thing to take into account is that to reduce the chances of double counting birds, point-count locations should ideally be separated by at least 275 yards, or 250 meters.

Now we get to the actual surveying. On a morning, or mornings, of your choice, walk or cycle your survey route(s) and conduct a series of five-minute unlimited-radius point counts.

The point count is a simple method frequently used to count birds. The birder conducting the count records all the birds seen or heard from a point-count station during a set period of time. The majority of birds will be heard rather than seen, which means that the point counter must be confident in his or her ability to identify songs. Point-count routes are conducted on a morning with good weather, in a predetermined order, always at the same time of day to make the data-collection contexts as similar as possible. If you are conducting yearly point counts, try to make them on approximately the same date each year. Although point counts require well-developed identification skills, many people find they enjoy the excitement of this approach to birding—and really improve their skills at the same time.

I am going to suggest to you a simplified system for counting birds in your patch that is based on that used in "A Habitat-Based Point-Count Protocol for Terrestrial Birds, Emphasizing Washington and Oregon" by Huff, Bettinger, Ferguson, Brown, and Altman (published in 2000 by the United States Department of Agriculture Forest Service's Pacific Northwest Research Station).

The important thing with all this is to be consistent with your methodology. That matters more than anything else.

When conducting your point counts you should restrict your observation period to the time from sunrise until 10:00 A.M., during suitable weather. Surveys should not be conducted in the rain or in winds gusting to 20 miles an hour or more. In general, you should be able to complete at least ten and up to fifteen points in one morning.

Always do the counts in the same sequence. On arriving at each count point, allow a minute or two for everything to settle down and then start recording the birds you see and hear for a period of five minutes.

It can be nice to have a friend accompany you on your count route. They can keep a record of what you see or hear—but only one person, and always the same person, should take the actual bird census observations.

Try to record the following information:

Count conditions

- Date on which the count was performed and the name of the route being surveyed
- Visit number—is this the first, second, or third visit this season? (You should have a minimum of a seven-day interval between surveys—but it's fine to go back in a more relaxed fashion just to enjoy the birds on days in between.)

- Start and finish times for the route that day
- Weather conditions, including cloud cover: overcast (cloud cover greater than 90 percent), broken (cloud cover 50 to 90 percent), scattered (cloud cover 10 to 50 percent), clear (cloud cover less than 10 percent)
- Temperature and wind speed. For wind speed, you can just note "calm" or "moderate"—as anything above that will interfere with bird detection and your point counts should be deferred to another date under these conditions. If you cannot hear the birds, then you should probably not try to do the count.

Bird detection information

- The identification name/number of the count station.
- Start time for each count station
- The names of each species detected at each station; each species is entered only once per station.

Count any bird you see or hear during the observation period anywhere from the ground up to the highest vegetation; count any bird within the tree canopy but not flyovers. Estimate the number of individuals of each species detected. Count all birds detected at the point (except flyovers and flushes) without regard to distance from the point, but try not to include birds that you think will be counted at an adjacent point. As you arrived at the count

We see Red-winged Blackbirds everywhere, and they will be on most green birders' lists. Get too close and, like this chap, they will flash their epaulettes to warn you away.

point you may have flushed some birds from the area. Count these only if you are sure that you did not subsequently record them elsewhere.

Depending on the length and complexity of your routes you may need to do your point counts over a period of several mornings, but do try to get out early when the birds are most active, and make sure that the survey days are completed at comparable time periods—that is, don't go out at 5 A.M. one day and 8 A.M. the next. If you have trouble getting up, it is better to compromise and go out at 7 A.M. each time.

Seasonal surveys

For your seasonal surveys, you do not need to set up routes as for the snapshot census; instead focus on specific bird-rich sites within your patch. Depending on the nature of your local area, your fitness, and the amount of free time you have available for survey work, you may decide to select only one survey site or you may choose several. If you have a variety of habitats in your area, then you might want to survey a variety—for example, an urban park, a stretch of riverside, a sewage treatment plant, an area of open grassland, and a golf course. Pick a place, or places, that you visit regularly and know well.

In each of your selected survey sites, choose between five and fifteen survey points. The number will vary depending on the size and nature of the area you are studying but the points should be at least 275 yards apart from each other to avoid any chance of double counting birds.

Monitoring your sites four times a year would be ideal. Each survey may be done in a single day or be spread out over a few days within the counting period depending on the sort of land you are visiting and how long it takes to do a thorough job. The counting period you use for each season will depend on how far north or south you live. For example, a birder in Tucson might use January 15 to February 15 as the winter period, April 15 to May 15 for spring (covering spring migration/breeding), July 1 to 31 for summer, and September 1 to 30 for fall. Where I live, in Quebec, on the other hand, we might prefer to count between January 15 to February 15 for winter, May 15 to June 15 for spring, July 15 to August 15 for summer, and October 1 to 30 for fall. Whatever date ranges you select, be sure to use the same ones each year.

In survey sites of consistent and relatively dense habitat such as woodlands you may choose to conduct five-minute unlimited-radius point counts such as you did for the census routes. Relatively open and uniform environments, however, are better surveyed using a line transect method, in which you survey 200-yard transects for ten minutes each. A transect is a defined line across the area you are surveying. For a point count you stand still and count birds; for a transect you walk the line for the designated period of time. In both cases, count all the birds you hear and see (except for those that fly overhead).

Any monitoring project that is conducted over a number of years, as I hope yours will be, inevitably comes up against changes in the environment surrounding the monitored sites. Projects conducted in urban settings may encounter such changes more frequently than elsewhere. For example, one year you may have difficulty accessing sites due to land-use changes such as the conversion of public land to private land, the gating of residential neighborhoods, the expansion of roads, and new construction. These are just things we have to live with and adapt to. If it's a matter of restricted access you might be able to negotiate with the landowner to come onto the land, but if a building or a road has been erected then it's really too late. On the other hand, if you know that a change of use of some land you have been studying is being planned, then the information you have been collecting about the habitat and the important species that live there may well help to sway the opinions of the planning authorities and persuade them to modify the building plans or even halt them altogether. Birders who know their patches well are front-line troops in the war against habitat loss.

WHAT TO DO WITH YOUR DATA

First, familiarize yourself with the use of a spreadsheet. It isn't essential, but it will certainly make your job much easier when it comes to analyzing your information. Whether with your point counts, your snapshot surveys, or simply your day-to-day sightings lists, having an efficient tool like a spreadsheet to manipulate your findings is very helpful indeed.

There are some remarkably complex statistical methods for using the data that you gathered to estimate population densities of individual species. These are outside the scope of this book, but if you are interested in applying them, you can find plenty of information about them on the internet. On the other hand, anyone can make simple calculations of the number of species X in woodland area Y. A pencil and paper will suffice for that.

After your surveys you will have the following records:

- Total number of species seen along each of your routes or on your localized patch surveys
- The number of individuals of each of the species at each individual counting station
- The weather conditions and the type of habitat at each counting station

From these, you can compile lists of what species are to be found on your patch or routes at the time of year when the counts were conducted and the types of habitat they favor.

Keep your records and repeat the surveys each year. Remember to report the basic information on eBird. Over time you will build up a detailed picture of what is happening on your patch. You may also be able to tell if outside influences are affecting bird populations. Has the weather been unduly hot or cold, wet or dry? Has there been a road-widening scheme along the edge of the patch you monitor? Has a field been plowed that used to be pasture? Has logging activity broken up stands of forest? Look back over your recorded observations and see if you can determine how the birds responded to these changes.

WHAT YOU CAN LEARN

I have asked many of the same questions that you will be asking about your local birds. Through the kinds of processes described in this chapter, I have learned all kinds of interesting things:

- Some friends and I established that Red-bellied Woodpeckers have not only been present in the past four years, considerably to the north of their traditional range, but have been pairing off and are probably nesting—a splendid addition to the local checklist of species.
- I knew that Red-shouldered Hawks were raising young on my patch and, from information given by a fellow birder and from the loud calling of a flock of crows, I was able to find and photograph the nest at the top of a shagbark hickory tree in a dense and almost inaccessible part of the arboretum. The parent birds were not impressed by my presence and warned me off in no uncertain terms!
- One day I watched a Warbling Vireo pop in and out of a gap in a woodland shrub at about head height. Peering in, I found a nest with an incubating bird sitting on the eggs. Needless to say, I stole quietly away but was well pleased at this confirmation of another breeding bird, and such a nice one too.
- There are breeding Barred and Short-eared Owls in parts of my patch that I only found because I have developed a feeling for the place by my close observation.

All of these things were interesting to learn and certainly well worth the effort of the studies. Sometimes, however, this kind of work benefits the birds as well. One year, through data I had collected on the birds in my patch, I was able to show that hay cutting on a couple of fields was timed too early, and ground-nesting Bobolinks, an endangered species hereabouts, were being adversely affected. As a result, measures have been taken to change the annual cycle of harvesting on those fields.

None of this was difficult or technically abstruse. This valuable information comes from observations that all birders can make once they get to know their patch thoroughly. It comes, at a basic level, from simply walking around and keeping your eyes and ears open. You can do it, too.

"Green birding is more than simply keeping a list of BIGBY birds. When you focus your energies on a local piece of land, you start to notice more than birds. You begin to pay closer attention to the local ecosystem. Prior to 2008, Indiana U regularly mowed the whole XC course, destroying nesting habitat for grassland birds in the process. Early in 2008 I lobbied IU to limit its mowing to just the XC running trails. The bulk of the XC course (40+ acres) has not been mowed since mid-May 2008, resulting in a big increase in nesting grassland birds like the Eastern Meadowlark. The presence of the Scissor-tailed Flycatcher in October was due in part to this change in mowing policy. Grasshoppers are a mainstay in this bird's diet, and the XC course has been loaded with grasshoppers since the mowing stopped."

—Bernie Sloan

Conservation

9

Most birders, like any other person who holds wildlife to be important, are deeply concerned about conservation, biodiversity, and the habitats in which creatures live. As we all know only too well, there is a frightening and growing loss of habitat around the world and even much of what remains is fragmented, so that its usefulness is diminished. Some leave it to others to do something about these problems, some contribute to environmental charities and activities, and a few get their hands dirty by actively working to conserve habitat where they can.

Green birders, in particular, with their heightened awareness of the effects our actions have on the environment and their close attention to a particular patch, are perhaps more sensitive than most to what needs to be done. We can (and perhaps should) be among those who "get their hands dirty."

But what can we do? What actions can a green birder take to help the cause of conservation—both locally and on a wider scale?

BE INFORMED

First, we can inform ourselves. Birders should know more than simply how to identify the birds around us on sight so that we can tick them off our lists. Learning how birds and habitat interact is interesting and satisfying—and that knowledge will allow us to work better in the cause of conservation.

Non-birders sometimes question why bird conservation is as important as we say it is and what difference it truly makes to the world at large. Who cares if we have a dozen more or less sparrows on the planet?

Avid birders and bird watchers know better. Bird and wildlife conservation is critical to the richness and diversity of the planet (which we share with more than 10,000 species of birds).

You can start by learning about the science of ecology. "Ecology" is a much-misused and much-misunderstood word which has come to be an

Despite what Hollywood has been telling us for years, the beautiful Bald Eagle (which may fly over many people's patches even if it doesn't land on them) has a rather pathetic "meep" for its call instead of the majestic scream we expect.

amorphous catch-all term with political overtones for anything vaguely green or environmental. Ecology is really the scientific study of the interactions of living things with their environment, and it is a rigorous academic discipline. Understanding the fundamentals of ecology will give you an understanding of the ecosystems in which birds live; you will then have the knowledge you need to go beyond that to act to ensure that the integrity of these ecosystems is maintained. Having this knowledge will allow you to speak with authority and be listened to.

BE AWARE

As local birders who are keeping a daily watch over the ecosystems we share with "our" birds, we are better placed than many to monitor and react to threats to the environment. Birders of all sorts—and, I would venture, green birders in particular—can be a powerful force for bird conservation, especially at the local level.

There are many things that birders can keep an eye on, including chronic or acute instances of pollution, habitat fragmentation or destruction, regional hunting regulations, changing populations of predators, plans for a road-widening scheme or a new subdivision or even the extension of a school sports field. All of these developments are connected to each other and can have often unexpected effects on birdlife on your patch. Even simple and unforeseen things such as a gradual rise in the numbers of feral cats as a consequence of home foreclosures can drive down local bird populations.

Knowing what the issues are, both globally and at the local level, will allow you to have the most effective impact on conservation activity. It is important that we all keep ourselves fully up-to-date about local wildlife issues and generally keep up with bird-related information. Use the internet, read newspapers, and check in regularly at local and national conservation discussion groups. This need not take inordinate amounts of our time, simply it means taking an intelligent interest in the world about us. We can achieve nothing if we don't know what is going on.

Being aware of local conservation issues and pressures helps us to play our own small part in keeping our local bird populations healthy. It also adds a layer of additional interest to our pastime of green birding.

BE AN ADVOCATE

If you are aware of a threat to a field, marsh, or area of forest, don't keep it to yourself. Try to find out as much as you can about who or what is responsible and then seek out other local environmental groups who might wish to know

The Yellow-eyed Junco is another of those elusive species that are found only in limited areas down near the Mexican border. But if that's where you are birding, you are going to enjoy having them with you.

about the problem—or who might already be aware of it and be able to point you toward ways you can help. The important thing is to speak out. Call your local radio station or newspaper; write letters to the press; post messages on local, regional, and national online message boards; and get the word out. We all have a responsibility as birders and people who care about habitat preservation to speak out. Don't let your silence cause damage to the environment.

Remember also that damage to habitat is not always malicious or profit-driven. Often it can be due to sheer ignorance; suggesting to those responsible for actual or potential damage that an alternative process would be less harmful may even be met with thanks. Even developers can be people who like birds.

JOIN WITH OTHERS

Of course, you can't do it all by yourself—nor should you try. Most towns have a local organization, often more than one, that works for conservation. Consider joining them and lending your voice and your services, because the ability to effect change lies in numbers. Many of these organizations are run by very experienced and knowledgeable people and they also are involved in bird research and rehabilitation in addition to more direct conservation projects.

These organizations often need volunteers. Many people give money and vocal support, but few get out there cleaning clogged waterways, lobbying decision makers, publishing newsletters, and managing websites. Get involved, meet other people in your area who feel as you do, and ensure that your patch remains a place where birds will be enjoyed by future generations.

In Canada, green birders can join Nature Canada, the Canadian partner of BirdLife International; together with Bird Studies Canada they launched the Important Bird Areas Program in 1996. Now there are around 600 IBAs across Canada. In the United States, similar work is done by the Audubon Society, among others, and in Britain you can join the Royal Society for the Protection of Birds (RSPB). Most of these organizations will have a local chapter in your area; they do good work. In addition, they are established organizations, and local and national authorities will listen to the information they provide.

Groups such as these, working at both the national and the local level, are key movers promoting bird conservation. They promote science-based, site-specific conservation for birds and habitat.

TAKE THE INITIATIVE

There are many small things that you can do yourself. We have already spoken about making your garden a wildlife-friendly place, however small it is; make an effort to grow native plants that provide fruit or seeds and provide shelter from weather and predators.

A pile of old logs may look unimpressive, but it will be filled with insects that attract small birds. Don't pass it by! I once got to watch nearly a dozen Winter Wrens scurrying about after insects in this particular pile.

Parts of your patch may be suitable for management activity by you and your friends—not every plot of land is private. Is your local park managed by people who are too neat and who think that every fallen twig or leaf must be tidied away? Woodland is supposed to have fallen branches and leaves; decaying wood and other dead plant material provide habitat for the insects that migratory birds depend on. Encourage the owners and managers of the places that you go birding in to leave as much dead plant material as possible on the land.

On my own patch, a great heap of logs lay for many years in a field. Some people thought it was an eyesore and wanted to have it removed. In actuality, as the heap decayed and became overgrown with vegetation it positively hummed with insects and was quite a magnet for many species of birds. Fortunately, we were able to point this out to the people who were planning to clear it away and they agreed to leave it alone. I can tell you that the birds are thankful—as are the small squirrels, chipmunks, and mice whose survival it also supports.

There is a particular dearth of habitat in most regions that is suitable for grassland bird species. Preserving grassland is a difficult task because almost any area of land that is not covered in trees or buildings is seen as fair game for farmers. Nevertheless, agriculture is in retreat in North America today and more and more formerly productive areas of arable land or pasture are being abandoned for economic reasons. Maybe you know of fields in your area that are like this? You can contact the landowners and suggest to them ways that the land could be restored for grassland species to return to. It needn't cost the landowner money, and you may well be surprised to learn that many farmers, municipalities, and other landowners with fallow plots on their hands are pleased and interested to learn how it can be improved for wildlife. Not everyone is a rabid agribusinessman only interested in the profit motive. These tracts of land are out there—they just need someone like you and the owner to recognize their worth and work to manage them.

Pay attention to areas of woodland as well. It is very important that woodland not be broken up by development and logging. It is also important to try to maintain a well-developed understory that includes a good mixture of woody and herbaceous vegetation, providing the necessary resources for as wide a selection of woodland birds as possible. Watch for the removal of this understory. Often this may happen because the landowner deliberately clears it out, preferring an open feeling in the woodland. In other cases it may be due to too high a population of browsing animals such as wild deer. Huge areas of forested land in the past twenty or thirty years have lost large numbers of birds simply because the people that used to hunt deer no longer do so. I don't intend to get into a discussion about the rights and wrongs of hunting, but it is an observable fact that if deer populations are not reduced in some way, they increase to the level that the woodlands and forests they live in effectively have no bird-holding understory. Sadly, many vociferous members of the public can't bear to think of "Bambi" being managed in any way and then close their eyes to the wider implications of their choices. In some places where a deer management policy has been proposed the opposition has been powerful. Ultimately this problem will be solved by education. Write to your local paper or get interviewed on a TV or radio station and point out that good management benefits all species, birds as well as deer. If you have a well-respected conservation group behind you, your argument will be that much more effective.

By using our local knowledge of the birds on our patch we can be part of the solution by being sensitive to current or planned changes and making sure that problematic ones are avoided, rerouted, or modified in some way. Very few developers really *want* to damage the environment, but they simply don't know how to avoid doing so. Help them, help yourself, and help the birds by speaking out and by working with others to manage, maintain, and even improve bird habitat.

The Last Word

Whether novice birder or hardened enthusiast with years of experience, you should now have a better idea of what being a green birder means. You have the tools to help you become the expert birder on your local patch and to have a go at the challenges of everything from a "Big Foot Hour" to a "Bigby." You can start to manage your garden to encourage the birds to come to you in greater numbers. And you can begin to study the birds on your patch in greater depth, through citizen science projects and independent research.

Turning from far-ranging traditional birding to local, self-powered green birding has changed my appreciation of the wildlife that I live with. I hope it will do the same for you.

I wish you some good (green) birding in the years ahead.

This Hudsonian Godwit is a true rarity; I dropped everything to track it down when it was reported, of all places, right near the edge of my patch—and just outside the serendipitously named town of Hudson!

Index

Page numbers in italics indicate illustrations and sidebars.